Intimacy on the Run

JEANETTE C. LAUER & ROBERT H. LAUER

Intimacy on the Run

Staying Close When So Much Keeps You Apart

DIMENSIONS
FOR LIVING
NASHVILLE

INTIMACY ON THE RUN:
STAYING CLOSE WHEN SO MUCH KEEPS YOU APART

This book is printed on recycled, acid-free paper.

Library of Congress Cataloging-in-Publication Data

Lauer, Jeanette C.
    Intimacy on the run : staying close when so much keeps you apart/ Jeanette C. Lauer & Robert H. Lauer.
      p. cm.
    ISBN 0-687-01770-X (alk. paper)
    1. Intimacy—Religious aspects—Christianity. 2. Time management—Religious aspects—Christianity. 3. Marriage—Religious aspects—Christianity. I. Lauer, Robert H. II. Title.
BV4597.53.I55L38   1996
248.8'44—dc20   96-19531
                                                CIP

96 97 98 99 00 01 02 03 04 05—10 9 8 7 6 5 4 3 2 1

MANUFACTURED IN THE UNITED STATES OF AMERICA

To those who have made our run faster, but have also added zest and laughter and love to the run:

Jon, Kathy, Julie, Jeffrey, Kate,
Jeff, Krista, Benjamin, and David

Contents

Intimacy on the Run

1

Caught in the Middle

"Therefore a man leaves his father and his mother and clings to his wife, and they become one flesh."

Genesis 2:24

> *"I am consistently overwhelmed by this heavy feeling that there is not enough time or enough of me to meet the demands of the day. My law firm expects me to work a ten-hour day, and my kids insist on my full attention once I get home. There is just nothing left for Paul and me. On my best days, I think that at least we're holding our own as a couple. But much of the time, I feel that we are losing ground."*
>
> *Amanda—lawyer, wife, and mother of three*

The Time Crunch

*W*e were recently bombarded by similar complaints from two very dissimilar groups. The first was a neighborhood play group that consisted of eleven preschoolers and their parents—five mothers and one father—all of whom were full-time homemakers. The second was a marriage support group that included eight dual-career couples. The groups were very different, but their complaints were essentially the same: "There just isn't enough time to do all we need and want to do."

Both groups complained of hectic schedules and demanding lifestyles. Sarah, a mother in the play group, told us that she spends an enormous amount of time

arranging and maintaining her kids' schedules. She esti-
mates that she puts several hundred miles on the car each
week driving her older children to and from school, to
Little League games, Scouts, dancing lessons, choir practice at church, and "to what seems like a birthday party
every week."

Tim, the only full-time male homemaker in the group,
shared Sarah's frustration. He had left his job as a medical
researcher three years earlier to assume the primary
responsibilities at home. His wife, Nancy, is an obstetri-
cian who works long and unpredictable hours. After several years of unsatisfactory child care, they decided that Tim
would take over the care of their three kids and would pursue his second career—writing—whenever he had time.
"What a joke!" Tim said.

> There's little time left for writing after I take care
> of the house and the kids. And Nancy and I sel-
> dom spend any time together—just the two of us.
> She's gone so much that, when she is home, she
> feels like she needs to give the kids every minute
> she has to spare.

Couples in the marriage support group expressed even
more frustration, if that's possible, than the full-time
homemakers. Paul, a real estate developer, confessed that
the most essential item in his life was his daily planner. "I
panic whenever I think about misplacing or losing my 'little black book,'" he told the group. "I sometimes feel like
it's my main link to sanity."

And Amanda, Paul's wife, told the group that she longed
for a good night's sleep:

> I bet that, over the last few years, I have averaged
> no more than five hours of sleep a night. I'm
> always tired and find myself fantasizing about
> sleep. In fact, my dream vacation is a week by

myself at a remote resort where I can sleep without interruption. At one point in my life, I would have thought this sounded like utter boredom, but now it sounds like heaven!

Too Many Choices, Too Many Demands

Why are we so rushed? Are we working longer hours than our parents did? Some of us are, of course. We may be workaholics or in professions that demand long hours. But the majority of us are probably not working longer hours at our jobs. In fact, surveys suggest that we are spending less time working than we did in the 1960s. Nevertheless, we feel rushed and even overwhelmed by demands on our time.

There are numerous explanations for the hurried and harried pace of contemporary life. It has been suggested that we have too many choices. Just think about your most recent visit to the grocery store: aisles of possibilities, thousands of things to choose from in hundreds of varieties and brands, including low calorie, reduced fat, or fat free. But choosing takes time as you decide between the healthiest, tastiest, or most economical product. It also can leave you feeling overwhelmed and rushed.

The goods and services available to us also reflect our busyness. Think about such things as the instant breakfast, the two-minute cup of soup for lunch, and the ready-in-a-jiffy microwavable gourmet dinner. And don't forget drive-in banking, postal service, and fast food; computerized grocery checkout; and speedy oil changes for your automobile—all designed to appeal to people in a hurry. Unfortunately, the net effect is to save you time so that you can do more things. As a result, life moves on ever more rapidly.

It's not just that you have too many choices, however. You also have more responsibilities. Contemporary lifestyle demands that, as a responsible person, you exercise, eat right, take charge of your health, stay politically and culturally current, raise the perfect child/children, make some contribution to your community, and so forth. The list seems endless.

And if that's not enough, something new is always being added to your list of responsibilities—the result of the increasing information glut that is transforming our global society. People are swamped with facts, advice, and opinions that are delivered ever more speedily by fax or E-mail. Moreover, this instant information often demands instant response. The pressure is on!

Finally, there is the reality of the dual-career household. About eight of ten married men and six of ten married women are in the labor force. Both partners work outside of the home in over half of all marriages, and these numbers are increasing. The cost of seemingly everything— houses, clothing, medical care, education—continues to increase and wages have not kept pace. As a result, many couples feel they need to have two paychecks if they are going to have what they believe they need or deserve. But when both spouses work, household chores and childcare are pushed into evenings or weekends, the hours couples and families have to spend together are limited, and the pace of life is accelerated.

Couples today are faced with the competing claims of pursuing a satisfying career, taking care of a home and children, and maintaining a vital intimate relationship. Not surprising, they feel caught in the middle, anxious, and even exhausted!

The Loser: Intimacy ✓

It doesn't seem to make much difference whether you are a dual-career couple or a couple where one spouse is a full-time homemaker. The situation is the same—too many demands and too little time. Unfortunately, this can be a lethal condition. The "hurry sickness" can affect your health. It has been blamed for a host of illnesses, including high blood pressure, heart disease, and depression.

The "hurry sickness" can also be lethal for marital intimacy. Research shows, for example, that dual-career couples experience more stress-related physical and psychological illnesses, generally lower levels of satisfaction with their marriages, and higher rates of divorce. Couples tend to leave their relationship until last. If there is any time and energy left—and there often isn't—then they attend to their relationship. After a busy day at work and caring for their children, Amanda told the support group: "There is just nothing left for Paul and me. On my best days, I think that at least we're holding our own as a couple. But most of the time, I feel that we are losing ground."

Paul and Amanda, along with other busy couples, often feel distanced from each other. They rarely talk together about themselves or their relationship; they often don't know what the other is thinking and feeling. They spend little time alone together; sex is less frequent than either prefers and may be rushed when it occurs. In sum, they are no longer as intimate as they once were. Their hurried lifestyle has corroded their relationship.

What Is Intimacy?

If busyness results in a loss of intimacy, exactly what have you lost? You have lost something of fundamental importance, for intimacy is the need that we all have to love and be loved, to belong to someone and have someone belong to us, to need and to be needed by someone. Intimacy is a close, vital relationship with another person and is the basis for personal fulfillment and well-being. When you are intimate with someone, your two lives are so intertwined that neither can be fully understood without reference to the other. Thus, marital intimacy means, in biblical terms, to become "one flesh."

Most individuals, of course, have a variety of intimate

relationships during their lifetime, primarily with friends and family. But marriage offers a unique kind of intimacy, an intimacy that can tie two people together for life and provide emotional sustenance in an impersonal, competitive world. Marriage allows you to develop a shared history of love, affection, and caring during happy as well as difficult times; and this shared history is the essence of intimacy.

It was this kind of intimacy that Todd and Maria, who had been married for twenty years, missed most after they divorced. And it was the desire to restore that intimacy that eventually brought them back together. During the two years that they were apart, Todd told us that he felt intimacy-deficient:

> I came to realize that we had too much invested in each other, too many things that we had done together. It just killed me to think of going to our children's weddings or seeing grandchildren or working for retirement without her. The problems that we had seemed less critical compared to this kind of loss. Fortunately, Maria felt the same way. It took us two years of loneliness, introspection, and intensive counseling before we were ready to remarry. But the happiness we share today was worth the work and the wait.

Tackling the Problem

You both need and deserve intimacy from marriage. The question is, Can you do anything to enhance the intimacy in your relationship despite your hectic lifestyle? And the answer is, Absolutely!

We begin with some essentials. First, you must make the *tough decision* to give high priority to your marriage. In chapter 2 we discuss why this is a necessary but also a difficult decision. In chapters 3 and 4 we examine two additional essentials—how to decide what the intimacy needs of each of you are and how to manage your time more effectively to meet those needs.

In chapters 5 through 7, we look at several sticky areas in most busy marriages—responsibility for household tasks, finding time for your relationship when you are surrounded by others, and allocating sufficient personal time in your schedule. We discuss how each of these areas can hinder as well as contribute to intimacy in your marriage. In the remaining chapters, 8 through 11, we furnish some *proven* techniques for building intimacy even while you are on the run. These techniques work. If you use them, they will enable you to experience the richness of intimacy despite the demands of a busy life.

About now you're probably saying: "All of this sounds great, but where am I going to find the time to read another book?" Your busy schedule was uppermost in our minds as we wrote this book. The chapters are short, divided into clearly labeled, manageable sections, and followed by a list of things you can do. So you can easily find help for a particular need even if you don't have enough time, at the moment, to read the book from cover to cover. In the long run, however, the time you spend in reading the entire book will be repaid in additional hours of rich intimacy.

Changing Directions: Your First Decision

"Be subject to one another out of reverence for Christ."
Ephesians 5:21

> *"Sometimes it feels like Mark is doing me a favor when he spends time with me instead of going into the office on weekends. I know his work is important to him, but why should I feel like I'm taking him away from what he'd really rather be doing?"*
>
> Karen—wife, homemaker, mother
>
> *"The biggest threat Jennie and I have faced in our marriage has come from our two careers. At one point, we each had excellent job opportunities in different parts of the country, and we vehemently disagreed over what to do. We finally decided to look for some place where we could both find satisfying work. When that didn't happen, we had a tough decision to make."*
>
> Curt—husband, college professor

We're All on the Fast Track

*I*t's safe to say that married life today is generally running on the fast track. There doesn't seem to be enough hours in the day to do all that needs to be done. And couples typically spend more time on their work, their kids, the yard, and perhaps even taking out the garbage than they do on each other. On a positive note, most couples recognize that their relationship gets shortchanged and want to correct the problem—if only they had more time. But that's the crux of the matter. You can't add to the hours in a day; you can't stretch the minutes to create some additional intimacy time. The only thing that you can do, if you want to avoid the "hurry sickness" and enhance your marital intimacy, is to change direction and start using your time in a different way.

A good place to start is to make the *tough decision* to give priority to your relationship. Now this *doesn't* mean that you won't work, that you won't spend time with family and friends, that you won't become involved in the lives of your church and community, that you won't take care of your spiritual and physical needs. It *does* mean, however, that you will give prime consideration to the quality of your relationship when you make decisions about how you spend your time, money, and energy. It means that you will reserve time for your spouse and that your marriage will not just get the leftovers—the time, if any, that is left at the end of the day. It means that you will strive to live as a loving unit rather than as two separate individuals whose lives only occasionally intersect.

Curt and Jennie had only been married six months when they had to decide which was more important— their marriage or their careers. Both were in the fortunate situation after graduate school of having excellent job offers. Unfortunately, the jobs were in different parts of the country. For weeks, they agonized over what they should do. Should they try a commuter marriage so that they each could have the job that they preferred? Or should they work in the same city with one taking the pre- ferred job and the other taking a position that, at the very best, would be a second or third choice? And if they decid- ed to work in the same city, which of them would take the preferred job?

Curt and Jennie finally decided against a commuter marriage. They knew that this kind of arrangement worked for some couples, but they felt that it wouldn't work for them. They wanted to share their lives on a daily basis and knew that a weekend marriage wouldn't permit this.

Their next decision concerned which one of them would sacrifice their personal preference. Would Curt accept the position of assistant professor at a West Coast university? Or would Jennie accept the offer to teach at an elite private school near the midwestern university where they had recently finished their graduate studies? After much discussion, they decided to go with Curt's offer because it involved more income and better advancement possibilities. They believed that Jennie would be able to find work in the new location. They also agreed that they would relocate when, and if, both found more attractive positions in the same city.

This was a tough decision for both Jennie and Curt. She had to cope with the loss of an appealing opportunity, while he had to deal with the guilt of depriving her of that opportunity. Still, they have no problem in justifying their decision. As Jennie says:

> In marriage, you make a commitment to each other. You put each other and your relationship above everything else. Certainly, I was disappointed that I had to turn down my job offer. But I know that the decision would have gone the other way if my offer had been better than Curt's. The point is, after a lot of agonizing, we realized that nothing is more important than our marriage and our commitment to each other.

Curt and Jennie have made an important decision—one that has already benefited their relationship. It's a decision, however, that Karen feels that her husband, Mark, has not yet made. Mark is an architect who, as Karen puts it, "is deeply in love with his job." She explains:

> Actually, his passion for his work is, in part, what attracted me to him in the first place. But now I'm jealous of it. He works ten hours a day, most weekends, too. And even when he's home, he's either hanging over his drawing board or thinking about his current project.

Karen often feels like an intruder in Mark's life, and she is convinced that she and their daughter are not a very high priority for him.

Why is it tough to give priority to your marriage? Let's look at a few things that can keep you from becoming one flesh.

Doing Battle with the Forces That Keep Us Apart

In the face of God's call to become one flesh, married couples battle a number of temptations and pressures to put other things before their relationship.

1. *Personal wants drive us.* Many couples today have the desire to succeed professionally, to accumulate material possessions, to have it all right now or as soon as possible, and to provide their children with every opportunity. You may have one or more similar desires. There's nothing wrong with these goals, but it may simply not be possible to reach all or any of them and still nurture your marriage.

This is the problem Mark is having. Mark loves Karen. He loves their daughter. He also loves his work. He acknowledges that he spends more hours than required at his job:

> My work means a great deal to me. But that's not all. It's the people who do more than what is expected who get ahead. I want to be one of the

best in my field. I want my wife and daughter to
be proud of my achievements. Is there anything
wrong with that?

No, there's nothing wrong with that. *Unless.* Unless it
keeps you from giving adequate time to your first responsibility—your marriage and your family. What will Mark
gain if he becomes the best in his field only to have Karen
say one day, as a woman recently said to us: "My marriage
is breaking up after thirty years, and the thing that makes
me the angriest is that my husband was never involved in
our relationship."

2. *Indebtedness can trap us.* Couples work hard to accumulate and then must keep on working to pay for their
accumulations. This happened to Allison and Steve. When
they married eight years ago, their economic future looked
rosy. Steve was prospering as a securities broker with a
large investment company and Allison had joined a promi-
nent law firm. They quickly purchased a large home and
furnished it lavishly—all on credit, of course. They rea-
soned that they could afford what they were buying—at
least, they could afford it in the next few years. So why
wait? That was before the birth of Melinda two years ago.
Now everything has changed—everything, that is, except
for the huge mortgage and credit payments. Steve told us:

> Allison puts in a long day. Her firm expects its
> junior associates to work ten to twelve hours a
> day, and that just doesn't leave enough time for
> Melinda. Allison vacillates between feeling
> guilty that she doesn't spend more hours with
> our daughter and feeling resentful and cheated
> because she's losing out on so much of Mindy's
> growing up. What free moments she has, she
> gives to Mindy and that leaves little time for us.
> Allison's greatest desire these days is to cut back
> on her hours at the law firm. But she can't

because we simply can't afford it. We'd lose everything without her full paycheck.

Allison and Steve feel trapped. They are victims of their own lifestyle and their neglect to give priority to their relationship over their desire for material comforts.

3. *Certain values, common in our culture, can subvert us.* "Work before play," right? In fact, isn't that a Christian value? Didn't Paul say anyone unwilling to work shouldn't eat (2 Thessalonians 3:10)? But even if work is a Christian virtue, allowing long hours at work to subvert the process of becoming one flesh is neither commendable nor healthy.

Is Mark to be congratulated for his career aspirations, his craving to become known as a topflight architect? Is Karen being unreasonable in her desire for Mark to cut back on his ambition and devote more time to her? We think not. Our value on becoming the best is more of a cultural than a biblical value. The point is not that it is unchristian to want to be, or to become, the best in your field. The point is that our Christian calling is to treat our marriage as sacred, a calling from God, a priority item on our list of things-I-must-do-with-my-life.

So given the pressures, given the temptations, where do you go from here? You make a decision to give your marriage high priority. It's a tough decision, but for the sake of being "one flesh," you must make it. The decision has four parts to it.

"We" Has Priority over "I"

First, you must decide that your relationship is your primary commitment. Only your commitment to God is greater. Marriage is ordained by God. Thus, one of the ways that you can demonstrate your Christian commitment is by giving sufficient care and attention to the spouse that God has given to you. In fact, Paul reminds us, the marital relationship is as sacred as that between Christ and his church (Ephesians 5:25-33). Just as Christ nurtures and cares for his church, husbands and wives are to nurture and protect their relationship.

Obviously, it is essential that both partners agree to this part of the decision. The woman who told us her thirty-year marriage was breaking up is an illustration of the devastation that can result when only one of the partners has made the marriage a primary commitment.

Your Needs Are as Important as Mine

The second part of your decision follows logically from the first part. Importance, incidentally, is measured by what something means to each of you. For example, although Curt and Jennie made their career decisions on the basis of the higher income and greater advancement opportunities in Curt's offer, such matters were not their first consideration. The first thing they talked about was how much the offers meant to each of them. They found their respective offers equally attractive. So the next step was to ask what other considerations—such as wages and other benefits, location, working conditions, future advancement—should be taken into account. It was only then that they decided to go with Curt's offer.

In contrast, Mark is not convinced that Karen's need for his committed presence with her is as important as his need to become the "best" in his field. He tells Karen, "What I'm doing, I'm doing for you and our daughter as well as for me." He feels that he is providing his family with all the benefits that money can buy and accuses her of being too dependent upon him for companionship.

When We Deal with Differences, Neither of Us May Get Our First Preference

Of course, Curt got his first preference. But if he and Jennie had both received job offers in the same city, they probably would have accepted them even though the jobs were not the first choice of either of them. That's part of your commitment to each other—the willingness to do something different from what you might do if you were single.

This third part of your decision is crucial because differences are inevitable, and the way you handle them is critical to the well-being of your relationship. We'll give you a method for effectively handling your differences in the next chapter. But for now, just keep in mind that you both need to feel a sense of fairness about the outcome.

Jennie felt that their decision was fair to her. Part of their agreement was that they would continue to look for other positions and would move again if they both found something attractive in the same city. And Curt agreed that a new offer would not have to involve as much money or opportunities for advancement as the one he accepted if Jennie found a good position.

Incidentally, work demands and career decisions are not the only kinds of situations that can confront you with the tough decision of giving your marriage priority. Whatever consumes your time—work, hobbies, a fitness program, volunteer work—can pose a challenge to your marital intimacy.

Raymond, for instance, is a volunteer junkie. He gets high on becoming involved in all kinds of causes and organizations. He is thrilled when someone asks him to participate in a project, and plunges enthusiastically into it. Marti, his wife of twenty-one years, has accommodated herself to his zest for volunteering by fashioning a life of her own. Their marriage is stable, but lackluster. They have affection for each other, but no sense of creating a shared history of joyous memories.

Raymond is doing what he believes he prefers to do. He is doing nothing wrong. On the contrary, he is making some important contributions to peoples' well-being. The cost of his contributions, however, is the richness of a one-flesh marriage.

We would make two observations about Raymond. First, if he chose to focus more on his marriage, the world would still survive. Whatever he now does would be picked up by other people and, even if it wasn't, he might make a better contribution by modeling a Christian marriage.

Second, if Raymond put the energy into his marriage that he puts into volunteering, he would find it to be a "more excellent way" (1 Corinthians 12:31) of life. That's why we said he is doing what he "believes" he prefers. People who achieve meaningful marital intimacy know that it is indeed one of God's richest gifts to us, well deserving to be compared to the richness of the relationship between Christ and his church. But such intimacy only comes to those who make the tough decision to give the marital relationship priority in their lives.

We Will View Compromise as a Win-Win Situation

The final part of your decision is to agree that all compromises you make as you resolve your differences are win-win situations. A young wife told us that she thinks compromise is vastly overrated. She called it a "lose-lose" proposition:

> It's like I want to go to Paris for our vacation and he wants to go to Rome. So we compromise and go to Yosemite. We both lose, because neither of us gets what we want.

You both lose, we pointed out to her, if the choice of a vacation spot is more important than your relationship. But if your relationship is more important, then you both win. Because you are together in that vacation.

Furthermore, you also strengthen your relationship when you agree to a compromise. This happens because of a basic social psychological principle: We are more invested in those things that cost us something. Organizations use this principle when they have entry requirements and payments. Jesus noted this principle when he pointed out that where your treasure is, there your heart will be also (Matthew 6:21). Note that he did *not* say, as many people believe, that if your heart is in something your treasure will be there also. Heart follows treasure. If something costs you, you will probably be more committed to it.

Clearly, compromise costs you something. In a marriage, you ultimately get far more than the cost, but the cost is certainly there. The point is, that the cost does not detract from your life. It adds immensely to it because it builds a stronger and more fulfilling marriage. So don't think of compromise in terms of "I lost." Think of it as, "We have won, so I have won."

Take Time To . . .

Beginning here, we will conclude each chapter with a list of practical things you can do to build intimacy in your relationship while you're on the run. Some of these we believe are essential, but many are optional. If they do nothing more than stimulate your own ideas about what can work for you, they are valuable. Consider them carefully, then select the ones you want to implement.

1. Together, agree to the four parts of the tough decision to give your marriage priority. Don't just say to each other, "Yes, we will do that." Repeat them aloud to each other as if they were wedding vows.

2. Seal your decision with a hug and a kiss. Most of us ended our marriage ceremony this way. Why not seal this

decision in the same way? Besides, hugging and kissing are good for building intimacy!

3. Think about, and share with each other, some times when you have given priority to your relationship over your personal preferences. It's helpful to recognize that, at times, you've already been doing what you are now overtly agreeing to do.

4. Pledge that you are going to work at finding some additional time for each other every day. You can't restructure your life immediately, but you can begin to make some changes. It's partly a matter of attitude. In subsequent chapters, we will provide ways to increase the intimacy in your marriage even while you are on the run. But the point here is to resolve that you are going to show how highly you prize your marriage by giving it sufficient time.

3

A Blueprint for Building Intimacy

"Therefore encourage one another and build up each other, as indeed you are doing."

1 Thessalonians 5:11

> *"When I first told her I wanted to go on an eight-day camping trip with three of my best friends from college, Sharon really blew her stack. She said that we only have three weeks of vacation time each year and should spend that time together. I tried to reassure her that my desire to take this trip was no reflection on her—it was just something that I needed to do for myself. She hasn't accepted that. I really want to go on the trip, but I don't know if it's worth the feeling I get from Sharon that I'm not being a good husband."*
>
> Sam—married for three years
>
> *"I could spend every waking minute running this business of mine. It's demanding. And, to be truthful, most of the time it's exciting. But I'm torn. I want to be at work and, at the same time, I want to be with my family. I know that a business can't give you a hug, or comfort you when you're down, or share a fun experience with you. I don't want to come to the end of my life and regret that I didn't spend more time on my marriage and kids."*
>
> Brian—husband, businessman, father

You've made the tough decision to give priority to your marriage. You are determined to build the kind of marriage that is lasting and enriching, a marriage that maximizes your well-being and joy in life, a marriage in which you know the pleasures of building up your mate and being, in turn, built up by your mate. Lofty goals! But how, given the many demands on your time, do you reach them? You need a plan—a blueprint for building a rewarding marriage. Granted this will take some time but, in the long run, an effective plan will save you countless hours. To be effective, your blueprint will require, first of all, a constructive method for resolving differences and, then, a clear sense of the intimacy needs of each of you.

Make Your Differences Work for You

Sam and Sharon had a serious problem. She resented his plan to spend eight days of their vacation time on a camping trip with his college buddies. Their arguments tended to go like this:

> Sharon: I need to be with you, and I feel that you are neglecting me.
>
> Sam: That's ridiculous. I'm not neglecting you. The problem is, you don't understand my needs.
>
> Sharon: I've always tried to understand you. *You* don't understand what I need.
>
> Sam: I would never neglect you. Why can't you see it from my point of view?

Notice the pattern? Each of them is using the method of attack and defend, attack and defend. That is, each attacks the other and defends his or her position. It's a common way to argue. It's also frustrating, time consuming, and ineffective. The first part of your blueprint therefore, shows you how to develop a practical, time-efficient, and intimacy-building method for dealing with your differences. The method has two parts.

Follow the James Principle

As James put it, we should "be quick to listen, slow to speak" (James 1:19). Part of the problem that Sam and Sharon were having was that each was trying to make a point without really listening to the other. As a result, they were wasting endless hours fighting without ever solving their problem.

Similarly, when Brian and Catherine came to us with marital problems, they seemed totally incapable of resolving their differences. At times, they got caught in the attack-defend method. More often, however, the problem was that Brian dominated the discussions and frequently interrupted Catherine with denials and efforts to clarify and correct her. Eventually, Catherine would give up trying to talk with him and retreat into a frustrated silence.

"In ten minutes," we told them, "we can teach you a better way." They were skeptical. But in ten minutes, we demonstrated the method and had them briefly practice it. Catherine beamed as she said, "That's the first time in fifteen years that I feel like Brian has actually listened to me." They were excited about using the method to begin rebuilding their marriage.

Here's the method.* As soon as you realize you are discussing a problem in which you are attacking and defend-

---

* This is a simple method, but it works. The basic idea has been used by counselors for some years. A slight variation of what we have suggested is an integral part of the PREP Program, which was developed at the University of Denver to train couples to deal more effectively with their differences.

ing, one of you must say, "Stop. Let's use the James principle." Then:

1. Decide who will begin, by flipping a coin if necessary.
2. The person who begins gives his or her point of view on the problem for a minute or two while the other listens. The listening spouse then paraphrases or repeats what the partner has said. If the one who has spoken is satisfied with the paraphrase, he or she continues.
3. After a few rounds, the roles are reversed—the listening spouse becomes the speaker and vice versa.
4. The process continues until each is satisfied that the other understands his or her position.

This process will work only if certain rules are followed. First, the listening spouse makes no comment on what is being said. He or she only tries to understand and articulate that understanding back to the speaker. Second, the speaking spouse draws no conclusions about the listening partner's motives or desires or needs. It would *not* be okay, for example, for Catherine to say to Brian: "You spend most of your time at work and don't consider my needs." It *would* be okay, however, to say something like: "When you spend so many hours at work, I feel like my needs aren't as important as yours," or "When you work so much, I feel like I'm not that important in your life."

Third, the speaking spouse only tries to explain, not to convince or solve anything. The point is neither to persuade your spouse to accept your point of view nor to resolve the problem. *The point is to understand and be understood,* to know how each other thinks and feels about the matter. When you have cleared the air and understand each other, you're ready for the next step—resolution.

Attack the Problem, Not Your Spouse

You are ready to solve the problem. And the problem is not your spouse (as implied in the attack-defend and other ineffective methods), but some issue or difference between you. Now that you understand each other's position on that issue or difference, resolve it with the following procedure:

1. If this is a recurring problem, talk about how you have dealt with it in the past. Obviously, your efforts in the past haven't worked, so you'll want to try something different this time.
2. Brainstorm to find as many ways to resolve the problem as possible. Remember that in brainstorming you write down each suggestion without criticizing or commenting on it. The point is to explore all of your options.
3. Each of you selects what you feel is the best idea and tells why you like it. You may even have some additional ideas or modifications of an idea that you would like to propose.
4. When you agree on the best idea, decide what you each will do to implement it.
5. Agree on a date for evaluating your efforts. If the idea worked, celebrate. If it didn't, select another from your list and go back to work.

After a couple of weeks of being in a total deadlock, Sam and Sharon finally agreed to try the "James principle" as an initial step in settling their differences. It was the first time that they had talked about the problem of Sam's proposed camping trip and really listened to each other. They also listened to themselves. Sharon realized, as she told Sam about her objections to his trip, that she felt threatened by his college friends. She told us:

I was afraid that this time together would make Sam wish that he were single and just one of the boys again. I totally forgot the depth of his commitment to me and acted like an insecure little girl. And in my jealousy and insecurity, I completely ignored how much this trip meant to him.

And similarly, when he finally listened to Sharon, Sam realized the depth of her feelings about his trip and the extent to which she felt excluded from his plans. Sam recalled:

Here I was going on and on about the trips that my friends and I had taken in college and never thinking that Sharon might feel like an outsider. When I really listened to her, I was able to reassure her of my love and that she was the most important person in my life.

Listening was an illuminating experience for Sam and Sharon. However, they still had to resolve the issue of whether Sam should take the trip. But this time instead of attacking each other, they attacked the problem. It only took one brainstorming session for them to come up with a workable solution: Sam shortened his camping trip to five days and met Sharon at a nearby resort, known as a paradise for lovers, for the next week and a half. They're delighted with the way their vacation turned out.

Whether you're confronting differences, trying to resolve an argument, or attempting to solve a problem, the James principle combined with an attack on the problem rather than your spouse will save you time, minimize your frustration, and build intimacy in the process. You're now halfway through the task of building your blueprint. Let's look at the other half—identifying the intimacy needs of each partner.

Determine Your Intimacy Needs

In order to build one another up (1 Thessalonians 5:11), you need to know each other's needs. To some extent, your needs will be different (the method we discussed above will be helpful in dealing with those differences). We all, for instance, require both privacy and intimacy. You and your spouse are not likely to require exactly the same amount of privacy and intimacy. And even if you do, you are not likely always to need them at the same time. That's why marriage is sometimes like trying to synchronize two watches that run at different rates.

Nevertheless, you should know what each other's important needs are. You can do this by engaging in three exercises: observe, reflect, and plan.

Step 1: Observe

We feel privileged to be making a career out of observing marriages. It is generally exciting and challenging, sometimes sad and frustrating, but always stimulating. And it has greatly enriched our own marriage as we learn from others how to (and how not to) build an intimate relationship. You can do the same on a smaller scale with two or three couples you know.

Identify with your spouse several couples that model the kind of intimacy you would like to have in your marriage. You may know them well or you may just have casually observed them. They may be older or younger than you. The important thing is that they have qualities that you admire. Perhaps your parents' marriage is one of them. A number of couples have told us that they feel blessed to have grown up in a home where their parents really loved each other. "They've been married over forty years," one young woman said, "and you can tell how much they still care about each other and how much they enjoy doing things together."

After you have identified these couples, list the behaviors that make these model marriages for you. Couples who have done this exercise have noted such things as:

- "We like the way they still touch each other after being married for so long. You can tell that they really love one another."
- "They seem so supportive of each other. They act like each other's most enthusiastic cheerleader."
- "We saw them having dinner at a restaurant last week, and they really looked interested in each other. We also loved the way that they laughed together."
- "My wife's grandparents have provided our number one model of a wonderful marriage. Probably the thing we cherish the most is the way that they look at one another with great love and caring. It just warms our hearts."

Once you have a list of qualities that you admire, talk about what they each mean to you. Why are they important? How can you develop more of these qualities in your own marriage?

If you have time, spend a few hours with one or more of the couples. Invite them over for dinner or out to dinner. Tell them what you admire about their marriage and ask how they developed such a relationship. This experience could be the most interesting and illuminating part of your observation.

Step 2: Reflect

The second exercise focuses on you and your intimacy needs. You probably expressed some of these needs in the first exercise when you talked about the qualities that you admired in other couples. But now it's time to be more specific and concrete about your intimacy needs. As a first step, each of you, individually, should complete the survey below.

> ## A Survey of My Intimacy Needs
> *The following seven statements reflect experiences that are important to intimacy. Read them carefully, then decide if you want to add something that is important to your personal intimacy needs. When you are satisfied that the list adequately expresses what intimacy means to you, rate each of the items on a scale from one to ten, where one means "I am completely dissatisfied with this aspect of our intimacy" and ten means "I am completely satisfied with this aspect of our intimacy."*
>
> I feel intimate with you when
> 1. we spend time together.
> 2. we engage in meaningful communication.
> 3. you express affection for me.
> 4. I feel cared about and cared for by you.
> 5. our sexual relationship is good.
> 6. I feel that you are committed to me.
> 7. I share pleasurable experiences with you.

After you have finished, make a list of several specific actions or activities that would improve your ratings in each area, even in those areas where you already have high ratings. You may want to include some of the techniques your model couples use in developing intimacy in their marriages. But don't limit yourself to these; loosen the reins on your imagination and be creative.

A caveat: Don't omit something from your list merely because you think it is impractical or because you think your spouse will never do it. We have heard spouses lose out on some real possibilities for enhancing intimacy with these kinds of excuses:

- "A weekly date would be great, but we don't have the time. It just can't happen."

- "I would love for John to come home and tell me about his day at work. But I know him. He simply won't do it."
- "I would like to have sex more often, but I know she has neither the time nor the desire."

Remember, at this point you are not trying to determine what is practical but rather what is desirable. How is your spouse ever going to know what your intimacy needs are if you omit from your list anything that sounds impractical or impossible to you?

By the time you have finished this personal survey, you should have a list of specific things that can be done to meet your intimacy needs and enhance the quality of your marriage. Now you are ready for the final exercise.

Step 3: Plan

This is the time for you and your spouse to discuss the results of the second exercise and to compare lists. First, talk openly about the results of the survey. This may not be easy for you because no person likes to hear that he or she is not fully meeting the needs of a spouse. But try not to be defensive. And, if you find that your emotions are getting in the way of really hearing one another, stop and use the James principle until you both come to an understanding of what the problems are.

After you feel that you each understand the intimacy needs of the other, decide which problem areas to tackle immediately. We recommend that each of you identify the area of intimacy needs that you would like your spouse to work on first. Then each use your spouse's list of specific behaviors as a starting point. We also recommend that you discuss whether you both feel comfortable with the items on the list. That is, you may have something on your list that your spouse may not be comfortable doing. Put an "x" beside any such item.

For example, Barry loves to water-ski, and one of the things he wants is for Pam to water-ski with him. The experience is so important to him that he really feels that she should share it if she is to know him completely. But Pam doesn't swim and is not comfortable on the water even if she wears a life jacket. Barry rightly put the item on his list. Pam rightly told him she would not be comfortable doing it.

When Barry pressed Pam to try waterskiing at least once, she grew irritated with him. Before the discussion became too heated, however, they decided to use the James principle and problem-solving method. As a result, Barry fully understood Pam's fear of water for the first time and wanted to drop the item from his list altogether. But Pam suggested that they brainstorm for another option. In the end, they came up with a compromise: Pam would go with Barry and sit on the beach—an activity that she loves—and watch him ski. He, in turn, would spend less time on the water and more with her on the beach. The "x" remains beside the item, "water-ski with me," but they have a new item— "go to the lake together for waterskiing and relaxing on the beach."

Incidentally, it's best to put an "x" beside the item rather than erase it, because you may change your mind at some point in the future. Pam may learn how to swim one day and decide she'd like to try waterskiing after all. What is out of the question today may be possible or even desirable in a few years.

The second part of this exercise is to decide which items on the list are practical *in terms of your present life circumstances.* In other words, decide which ones you can implement now as opposed to those that might be practical in the future. For Barry and Pam, "go with me to Italy" was not a shared experience that was financially practical. But it could be at some future date. Put an "m" beside such items, indicating that they are a "maybe" for the future.

You now have a better understanding of your spouse's intimacy needs and a list of activities with which you both are comfortable and that you have agreed are practical. Don't try to implement too many new activities at once. You don't want to strain an already busy schedule with a whole list of new activities. Rather, try one or two. Periodically, review your progress and decide whether it's time to work on another problem area or to add another item to your intimacy repertoire. If you do this, you're well on your way to meeting your, and your spouse's, intimacy needs in an exciting new way.

Take Time To . . .

1. Invite a couple whose marriage you admire to dinner. Talk about their experiences and marital growth.

2. Practice the James principle, using a topic about which you have a minor disagreement.

3. Tell your spouse about an incident from your childhood that has helped make you the person that you are today.

4. Treat your spouse to a secondhand experience. Choose some activity in your life that your spouse is not likely to participate in but that is important in making you the person you are today. Describe or demonstrate the activity and relate why it is so important to you.

4

Time: Taming the Devouring Monster

"For everything there is a season, and a time for every matter under heaven."

Ecclesiastes 3:1

"I realize that Jerry has a lot to do. But who doesn't? It seems to me that if you don't have time for your marriage, there's something very wrong with your life. Jerry says he's working hard for our future. Well, I told him I need to live in the present not just in the future and, that if we don't enjoy each other now, we may not have a future together. That got his attention, and we're getting our marriage back on track at last."

Stacy—wife of two years

"Work. Kids. Our parents. The house. Church. Sometimes I think I could spend all of my time on any one of them. There doesn't seem to be any time left over for Carol and me, or for any personal interests I might have. I don't see any way to manage my time so that I can do all of the things I have to do, much less some of the things I'd like to do."

Kevin—husband, sales manager, father

There may be "a time for every matter under heaven" (Ecclesiastes 3:1), but it's likely that you feel like Kevin— there simply isn't enough time for you to handle all the things you must do and want to do each day. Yet, most of us are in the same boat. We are allotted the same number of hours in a day and have more demands and duties heaped upon us than we have time to handle. Or so we think. But there *are* people who manage this much and more in a day. How do they do it?

Clearly, those who deal effectively with all the demands of life must have good time-management skills. Someone has called time a "devouring monster." You probably have many moments when you agree. However, we are not only told that there is a time for every matter under heaven, but also that we are to tame that monster, to make "the most of the time" (Ephesians 5:16).

There are four things you can do to make the most of your time.

Think of Time as Your Ally

This may sound strange to you. You probably think of time as the enemy, as that which is always in short supply. If the writer of Ecclesiastes is correct, if God assures us that there is a time for every matter, then you must have enough time for all you need to do in life. You may not have time for all you *think* you need to do. You may not even have time for all you would *like* to do. But you do have the time to complete whatever God has called you to do.

So think of time as your ally, as God's gift to you. Thinking of time as your ally rather than as your enemy or as a serious shortage in your life can achieve something very important: It can help you to feel more fulfilled and more relaxed as you structure your time. These feelings come from the sense that you are doing, and have the time to do, God's bidding.

The point is that when you think of time as the enemy, you are likely to feel the kind of time pressure that takes a toll on your relationships. Jerry learned this when he was trying to juggle a full-time job, a university graduate program, and a new wife. He acted like, and felt like, a man pulled in too many directions. Before Jerry learned how to deal with the demands on his time, one of Stacy's complaints was the feeling that she usually got less than all of him, even when they were together:

> We were only married for a year when I began to feel really distressed. I always hear about men complaining that their wives don't have sex with them often enough. But I was the one with that complaint in our marriage. Jerry would go for two or three weeks without showing any sexual desire. I was feeling emotionally deprived and frustrated.

Even worse, however, there were stretches of three or four days when Jerry would hardly talk to me. He was always either studying or rushing off to class or to work. And even when he did talk to me, I had the feeling that he was preoccupied with other things.

When Stacy finally got Jerry's attention by suggesting that their marriage was in real trouble, they began to deal with the problem. After some discussion, they agreed that Jerry would take off one night a week and devote it to Stacy. He would not think about work or school, but would enjoy being with his wife. She, in turn, would expect no more than this one night a week for the next nine months—the time it would take to finish his master's degree.

Did taking a night off increase Jerry's sense of time pressure? At first, he feared it might. He was pleasantly surprised, however, to discover that he felt less time pressure than before:

> The first couple of weeks were a little hard. But we kept at it, and I began to look forward to our night together. I knew I had been neglecting

Stacy, so I felt good about our marriage getting back on track. And the break actually made me more efficient at work and school, so I haven't lost ground there. I never thought that adding something to my schedule could possibly help, but it did.

Jerry also dropped a few things from his schedule, mainly some recreational time at his computer and a couple of favorite television programs. But he gained a new sense of relaxed fulfillment. Time has become his ally, enabling him to do those things that are truly important and necessary at this point in his life.

Run Your Marriage Like a Business

We don't want to push the analogy too far, but many of the time-management techniques that business people use to organize their work are just as helpful in family life. In business, time is money. In marriage, time is intimacy.

Be a Good Time Manager

The following techniques are useful not just for efficiency, but also for intimacy. Some may save you hours and some may save only minutes, but every minute saved means more time available for developing intimacy.

1. *Make a list of what needs to be done.* You may think you know what needs to be done, you just lack the time to do it. But listen to the testimony of a young husband who had a new job:

> At first, I felt I was going crazy. I had a million things whirling around in my mind and constant anxiety that I was going to forget something. So I started making a list of things I needed to do immediately or in the near future. I made one list

for work and one for home. Just writing things down reduced my anxiety and made each day seem much more manageable. I gained a reputation for being one of the most organized managers in my office. And I was a lot more relaxed at home because I felt I had things under control.

Among other things, a list can help you organize tasks so that you are more time-efficient in dealing with them. A wife told us that she always does several errands at a single outing. She lists the places she needs to go and, then, decides on the best route to take to minimize her driving time.

2. *Prioritize.* Prioritizing helps you accept time as your ally—low-priority items may or may not get done. Repeatedly remind yourself that what is necessary for you is not to do everything you feel you ought to do or would like to do, but to do those things that, in your understanding of God's calling, are priority items for you.

One of Kevin's problems is that he does not prioritize by asking what is important in the light of God's calling for him. He does prioritize, however, and work is his first priority. "If I don't work, we don't eat" is his explanation. It's really a rationalization. Kevin's burning ambition is to be the best sales manager his company has ever had. To achieve that goal, he is working far more hours than are necessary.

We do not believe that God has called anyone to be the best of anything at the expense of the marriage and family. Until Kevin accepts new priorities in his life, he will continue to feel the pressure of time, the frustration of too many demands, and the experience of a mediocre marriage.

3. *Set time limits.* Parkinson's Law states that work expands to fill the time available for its completion. You need not be rigid about time limits, but if you don't at least have a limit in mind you may find yourself spending

far more time than necessary on some tasks. Therefore setting time limits on some tasks is a good idea.

Linda and her husband were determined to spend at least thirty minutes every evening together. They felt that it was essential to the vitality of their relationship to reconnect at the end of a busy day. But Linda had difficulties reserving this time because she was captive to a very needy friend. Sue, who had been her best friend since high school, was having trouble recovering from a painful divorce, and she called Linda nearly every evening after dinner. Linda told us:

> Sue just wanted to talk. She needed me to listen and to support her. But she talked on and on. Sometimes I was on the phone with her for two hours. I got nervous and impatient, but I still hated to cut her off. Unfortunately, by the time she hung up, there was no time left for John and me.

Linda took her friendship with Sue very seriously, but she had to set limits on their telephone conversations if she was going to have the necessary time with John—her first priority. She finally began limiting their calls by saying to Sue: "It's great to hear from you. I've only got ten minutes to talk, but they're all yours." And then when the ten minutes were up, she would conclude the call. This wasn't easy for Linda, but it allowed her both to support Sue and attend to her marriage.

4. *Use the Premack principle.* This psychological principle states that you should do things in order from the least to the most desirable. Doing the task you dislike the most gets it out of the way. And by doing a more desirable one next, you are, in effect, rewarding yourself for completing the earlier one. Following this principle, therefore, will make you more effective and efficient in doing tasks that you dislike.

Keep in mind the purpose of the Premack principle. It is only a tool to help you whip through the undesirable tasks of the day and allow you more time to concentrate on the desirable—in this case, your marriage. Don't do what many people do (perhaps they're masochists at heart) and have so many undesirable tasks on your daily schedule that you never get around to the things that you really want to do.

5. *On occasion, do two tasks at once.* You shouldn't always try to do two things at once. For instance, you certainly don't want to think about your next day's business meeting while making love. But many things can be done in tandem. A long telephone cord permits you to talk while you cook. You can sew or repair things while watching television. You can use the time spent waiting in lines or offices to chart the next day's activities or plan something special for your spouse. Exercise together, and, with some kinds of exercise at least, you can use the time for intimate talk.

6. *Learn to avoid time traps.* There are some classic ways to waste time. One is procrastination. You are more likely to procrastinate on tasks you dislike; if you don't have a more agreeable task to do afterward, you can use the Premack principle by rewarding yourself in some way for completing the disliked task (read, relax in the sun, enjoy a treat).

Perfectionism is another time trap. Is it worthwhile to spend the extra time making your house absolutely spotless? Should you take the time to refinish an old table because it has a small stain on it? Is it better to pull the weeds out of the flower bed than to take a walk together? We're not saying that there is a single right answer to every such question. We suggest, however, that you ask such questions and see whether you can compromise some of your standards in order to give time to each other.

Finally, avoid the common trap of wasting time making minor decisions. How many times have you become frustrated trying to decide which movie you want to see, or which restaurant you'd like to go to, or what you want to do Friday night? One way to deal with this is to take turns making the decision, with the other spouse either having or not having veto power (in the former case, the spouse who vetoes a suggestion must come up with an alternative).

You can also turn minor decision making into a game. We know a couple who handle the question of where to eat out by each of them writing down the names of five restaurants on separate pieces of paper. They put the pieces into a hat, shake them, and draw out one at a time. The last one they draw is the place they go to that evening.

7. *Get help.* In business, they call this delegating. We simply say, get help. If you can afford it, hire someone to mow your grass or clean your house. Look into the possibility of having someone cook your dinners during the week. Instead of spending hours at a garage or service station, let a company come to your home to tune up your car. If you can't afford these services, look for some ways you can share tasks with friends or neighbors. And, if you have children, make sure they have household tasks. Even preschoolers can pick up their own toys. Older children can assume greater responsibilities.

Should You Be Doing Something More?

Kevin's problem is not just that he has many demands on his time. He is also vexed by the feeling that, because of those demands, he should always be doing something more. At work, he knows and practices most of the time-management techniques discussed above. He regards himself as a good businessman. He would agree that there is value in applying business principles to his home and marriage. But he has yet to see that good business practices involve more than the work itself. Astute business leaders know the value of cultivating close relationships through such things as office parties, company picnics, bowling teams, and so on. And the truly successful leaders, those who have succeeded in business at the same time they have built rich, fulfilling lives, know how vital it is to maintain strong intimate relations as well as nurture their personal well-being.

In other words, when we say to run your marriage like a business we do not mean to make it all work and no play. As Carol points out, Kevin has a problem relaxing:

> We were sitting on the couch one Sunday afternoon just reading the paper. I was really enjoying it. I shared some things I read with Kevin, and he shared some with me. For me, it was a good time, an intimate time. Then Kevin suddenly put down his paper and said, "I feel like we're so lazy, just wasting time this way. We ought to be doing something."

As far as Carol was concerned, they *were* doing something. They were together, they were sharing, they were relaxing. In fact, the point of the time-management techniques is precisely to give you such moments when you can just be together doing something you enjoy. Don't learn and practice these techniques so that you can meet ever more demands and take on increasing responsibilities. Instead, use them to create more intimate moments.

Protect Your Calendar

If you don't control your calendar, you can be sure that others will. For busy couples, a written calendar (rather than one that you try to keep in your mind) is imperative. It is also essential that you use it to *act* and not merely to react to all the demands and requests that come to you.

Too many couples make the mistake of looking at their calendars after everything else is penciled in and asking, where can we fit in some time for ourselves? And frequently when you expect to have some time together on the weekend, a request or invitation comes in and you suddenly have no free time at all.

You make time your ally when you pencil in your intimacy times first. This allows you to say "no" to some requests that you otherwise might accept. A professional man, who has numerous requests for night as well as daytime meetings, finds this approach invaluable:

> I write "MAR" on my calendar for weeks in advance. MAR are my wife's initials. When someone asks if I can do something on a night when MAR is written down, I tell them no, I am already engaged for that night. I don't have to offer any further explanation. And I feel comfortable saying this, because my marriage is as important as my work. If I didn't have her initials written down, however, I would not be comfortable refusing someone's request. Then my calendar would be full, and Michelle and I would rarely if ever have an evening together.

Social as well as work-related requests can consume your calendar. When Jerry and Stacy agreed to take one night off to be together, they soon faced a question: What should we do if some friends invite us out? They realized that friendships are important. They also realized that time with friends is not the same as couple time. They decided that they would always keep at least three nights a month for themselves. Those nights would be inviolate. Friends would be told that they were sorry, but they were already tied up for the evening.

Like time, your calendar is your ally. But it is only your ally if you use it to protect your intimacy time as well as to organize the demands and responsibilities in your life.

Practice Your "Intimacy Musts"

You used the exercises in the last chapter to identify your intimacy needs. We suggest you think of them as "intimacy musts," essentials for creating a fulfilling marriage. In order to satisfy your intimacy musts, you will need to be creative both in the use of your calendar and in the way you use your free time.

Schedule Both Regular and Irregular Intimacy Times

You should schedule intimacy times on your calendar at least a month in advance and for some things several months in advance. For instance, you may want to plan for some regular time together—a weekly date on Friday or Saturday evening and a daily time for sharing in the morning or evening. Reserve those times on your calendar. Don't worry if children or some unexpected event *occasionally* intrudes and deprives you of such times. Only God's time is completely inviolate.

You will also want to schedule time for special occasions. Jerry and Stacy enjoyed their weekly date so much that they both agreed they wanted to take an occasional weekend away. That required some planning:

> We looked at our calendar three months ahead, thought about all that was coming up at work or school, then chose a weekend to go away. We didn't know where we were going when we reserved the date on the calendar. We just wanted to be sure to keep that time free. It was fun to anticipate and plan for our trip. We not only enjoyed the weekend, we loved thinking about it and planning for it.

For something special, like a particular anniversary, you might even plan a year or two in advance. Putting it on your calendar encourages you to start saving, researching places, and arranging your life so that you can make the trip. Plus you have the joy and excitement of anticipating the special event.

Create Intimacy Times at Odd Moments

To fulfill your intimacy musts, put your imagination to work creating time together when there apparently isn't any available. We call these the "odd moments"—those times when you can squeeze in some time together even though you are otherwise occupied. For example, a couple told us that they make a daily love connection via the telephone. He calls her at her office, or she calls him at his. If they get through to each other, they spend just a few moments talking about how the day is going so far. If the spouse is unavailable, an "I love you" message is left on the voice mail.

Even Jerry and Stacy found some odd moments in their hectic schedules. As their marriage became stronger, Jerry and Stacy wanted more time together. One solution they came up with was for Jerry to accompany Stacy when she does her weekend errands. For example, Stacy must do her shopping on weekends. But Jerry both hates to shop and hates to give up his study time. So now they drive together to the shopping center, using that time to talk with each other. Then Jerry finds a chair in the mall and reads while Stacy does her shopping.

To create your own intimacy moments at times when you otherwise would not expect to have them, ask two questions. First, at what times during the day could I make a telephone call, or write a love note, or plan a surprise? Second, what are we now doing separately that could be done, at least partially, together? The important thing is to not get caught in the trap of thinking you have no alternatives, that there is no way you can create more intimacy time than you already have. In later chapters, you will find some additional ideas that you can use, but put your own creativity to work as well. No one can imagine better than you what would be pleasing and fulfilling for your marriage.

Take Time To . . .

1. Discuss together how you are spending your time. Ask yourselves: Are we giving sufficient time to our marriage and to the tasks that God has called us to do?

2. Make a to-do list for each busy day, listing the tasks in order of importance or the order that they can best be done.

3. Think about ways that you can find extra time in your day. Are you spending far too much time on certain tasks? If so, set a limit on how much time you are going to give to those tasks. Or if you are a perfectionist, lower your standards a bit.

4. Plan your calendar for the next three months and make certain that your time together is the first thing scheduled. And, then, stick to it as best you can.

5. Find an "odd moment" each day to let your spouse know how much you treasure him or her.

5

Who Tends the House?

"Then the LORD God said, 'It is not good that the man should be alone; I will make him a helper as his partner.'"

Genesis 2:18

"I'll tell you exactly how I feel. My annual income is twice as much as Laurel's. So as far as I'm concerned, it's only fair that she is responsible for the house. We've discussed the matter a lot, and I know she doesn't completely agree with me. But that's the way it is."

Scott—married for three years, physician

"I don't know whether we do the same amount of work around the house or not. We each do the things we prefer to do. Bill likes to cook, so he usually fixes the evening meals. And I like a clean house, so that's where I concentrate my efforts. Neither of us complains about what we do. It just isn't an issue for us."

Anne—wife, bookstore manager

---

*O*ne of the vexing problems that busy couples face is household tasks. As a wife put it: "There are times when I feel that I have put in a full day of work and earned some intimate moments with my husband. And, then, guess what? I remember that the laundry has to be done if we're going to have clean clothes to wear tomorrow."

For many couples, the problem is even more vexing because they haven't thought carefully about the order of creation. Genesis tells us that when God created woman, she was to be man's helper and partner. Eve was not created as a servant, nor as the one who was to have primary responsibility for the home while Adam roamed around taking care of the garden. In God's order of creation, men and women are partners. This suggests shared responsibility for managing a shared life. It sounds straightforward and fair. But working out the details of the partnership can be difficult, particularly when it comes to the issue of who does what around the house.

Warning! Housework Can Be Hazardous to Your Marital Health

When Scott and Laurel first talked to us, we raised the question of how, in view of the fact that both worked, they handled household tasks. There were a few moments of silence. Then Scott said, "It's no problem. We did debate that one a lot, but we finally have agreed to disagree." Laurel remained silent. But there was a look of disquiet on her face. "You don't look as if it's no longer a problem, Laurel," we observed. She responded slowly, as though she were trying to control her anger:

> We did disagree. We do disagree. But I don't see any solution. Scott insists that, because he earns far more than I do, I'll have to be responsible for the house. He says that's fair because he's contributing a lot more to our financial situation than I am.

Laurel shrugged and looked away. We urged them not to drop the subject. "You may be building a time bomb that will explode in the future," we warned. We encouraged Scott to rethink his position. Although Laurel's income as a registered nurse is not as great as his, she works as many hours a week as he does. So far, Scott hasn't budged. The issue is still a nettlesome one for them. And it is eroding the quality of their intimacy.

We haven't met many people like Scott who measure their marriage partnership in such crassly monetary terms. But we know a good many couples for whom the issue of household tasks is vexing. Although most people believe that marriage is a fifty-fifty proposition (we'll comment more on this idea later), only a minority of couples practice this when it comes to tending the house. National studies show that wives who work outside the home tend to spend twice as many hours in housework as do their husbands.

Thus, the reality in many marriages is that wives have fewer leisure hours than their husbands. Some, like Laurel, grimly try to accept their feelings of inequity. Some, like Phyllis, confront their husbands:

> I'd finally had it when Hank announced to me that he was taking a weeklong fishing trip in the Canadian backwoods. He was so excited that I didn't say anything at first. Instead, I stewed about it for a few hours. But then I couldn't restrain myself anymore and accused him of being unfair. He looked puzzled and asked what I meant. I told him that, since the birth of our second child last year, I felt I was doing more than my share around the house. Keeping up with housework, two children, and my job just overwhelmed me at times. And now he was going off by himself for a week and leaving it *all* for me to do. It just wasn't fair.
>
> As it turned out, it was a good thing Hank planned the trip. It forced us to work out some things that had been bothering me for a long time. Hank agreed that I had been carrying an extra load around the house. So now he's helping a lot more with the kids and household chores. I'm feeling much better about him and about life generally.

Note that Phyllis talked about "fairness." That's critical. For a marriage to be fulfilling, you each have to feel that the distribution of tasks is fair and that you really are partners.

Forget About Equality—Maintain Equity

While it is true that many people agree that equality is the ideal and should be practiced in marriage, we urge you to forget about equality and concentrate on *equity*. Equity is what Phyllis identified as important—a sense of fairness, a sense that you each are getting as much out of your relationship as you are putting into it. There are a number of reasons for focusing on equity rather than on equality.

Equality Is Like a Snipe Hunt

Striving for equality in marriage is like hunting for snipe. When we were growing up, it was a common practice for teenage boys to organize a hunt for snipe—a creature that didn't exist in the area where we lived. They would pick some unsuspecting fellow and invite him to the hunt. Equipped with flashlights and a bag to hold the quarry, they would send the victim out in search of snipe. Of course, no one ever saw or captured a snipe. And so the naive comrade was left alone, holding the proverbial bag. Equality in marriage is much the same. You don't really know what it looks like, and you are never able to capture it. Equality, in short, is an unrealistic goal.

For one thing, equality is often unattainable. There will be times when one or the other of you will have to assume a larger share of the household chores because of unusual circumstances. For example, one of you may be ill or have additional work and family responsibilities that consume your time.

Second, it follows that equality is one of those expectations that is bound to be thwarted at some point. If you expect your marriage to be a fifty-fifty proposition, you will inevitably be disappointed. What then should you expect? In our study of hundreds of long-term, happily married couples, we repeatedly heard the advice: Avoid the expectation of equality. "Go into marriage," urged a husband with a thirty-year marriage, "expecting, and willing, to give more than you get. In the long run, you'll get all you need and then some."

Third, if you insist on equality, you'll have to keep score. And that's a difficult assignment. What kind of values do you place on dissimilar tasks? Can an hour spent in balancing the checkbook possibly equate to an hour spent cleaning the grout in the bathroom? What if you enjoy some household tasks while your spouse hates them all? How can you measure which of you is more tired and needs more rest? Or suppose that you keep track of the exact number of hours you each spend on housework in a week. If it turns out that you spend an hour more than your spouse, are you being cheated? Or you may give yourself extra credit for certain things. Scott did this. His additional income, he insists, balances out the extra hours Laurel spends in housework. Scott does not think of himself as arbitrary or domineering. Rather he believes that he is building a marriage of equality.

Such carefully measured "equality" is not the biblical way, however. Paul, for example, could have easily claimed the privilege of apostleship and insisted on having his material needs supplied by those to whom he preached. But, he wrote to the Thessalonian Christians: "You remember our labor and toil, brothers and sisters; we worked night and day, so that we might not burden any of you while we proclaimed to you the gospel of God" (1 Thessalonians 2:9). Despite his revered status and his contributions to their spiritual well-being, Paul did not consider himself above doing manual labor while he was at Thessalonica. Translated into modern terms, this means that whatever your income or the status of your job, no one is above laundry, housecleaning, cooking, changing diapers, baby-sitting, and mowing the lawn. No task is the exclusive responsibility of one spouse. Marriage is a partnership.

Strive for Equity

In contrast to equality, equity means that you don't keep score; you just try to maintain a general feeling of fairness. Read again the statement by Anne at the beginning of this chapter. She and Bill both work. Some of what they do around the house is nontraditional. Neither has any idea of how many hours the other spends doing household tasks. And they have no problem because each feels that what is happening is fair. Fairness means that you are satisfied with the household division of labor. And you are more likely to attain the sense of fairness when you don't bring factors of income and privilege into the equation of deciding who does what. For example, Carl and Wendi have three small children. He is a high school principal and she is a housewife. You might assume that Wendi, because she is unemployed outside the home, would do all of the household chores. But Carl cooks most of the evening meals. He explains:

> Have you ever spent the day taking care of three small children? After only a couple of hours, I'm exhausted. So I know how Wendi feels most days. Anyway, I enjoy cooking. It's no big deal for me, and it relieves her of having one more chore during the day. She uses this time to bathe the kids and get them ready for an early bedtime following dinner. This frees up a couple of hours every evening for us to just be together as a couple.

How to Create Equity

If either you or your spouse feels a sense of unfairness in the household division of labor, don't despair. You *can* create equity.

1. *First, decide how you will measure fairness.* Avoid counting hours, income, and stress level—often the kind of things that go into measuring equality. Rather we suggest that you use a simple measure: How much free time does each of you have during an average day? Is there a significant difference? If so, does the difference reflect other important factors, such as the fact that one of you has a much more demanding job than the other? In other words, the first step is to decide whether there really is inequity. If there is, go on to the next step.

2. *Each of you suggest a way, that you prefer, to resolve the inequity.* For example, if your spouse has an hour more free time on an average day, what household task could he or she take over? Keep in mind that you don't necessarily have to balance out the hours exactly—either daily or weekly or monthly. You might want to ask your spouse to take on a chore that is onerous to you, in return for which you would gladly work a few hours a week more than he or she does. Or you might propose that your spouse accept a weekly chore that consumes a chunk of time that you value. Remember that equity is not necessarily equality. Equity means that you are satisfied with the division of labor.

3. *If you have difficulty coming to agreement, use the method we described in chapter 3 for resolving differences.* This method, which uses the James principle and a proven problem-solving technique, will enable you to build an equitable relationship in the shortest possible time and with minimal frustration.

Make Household Chores Enhance Your Intimacy

In the last chapter, we suggested you think of time as your ally. Now we're suggesting the same thing for household tasks. Think of ways your household tasks can work *for* your intimacy instead of against it. Ask yourselves the following questions.

What's the Spiritual Purpose of Washing Dishes?

The first way to use household chores is to define them as spiritual tasks. It may sound silly at first to think about a spiritual purpose in something like washing the dishes, but the point is a serious one.

What is your calling as a family member? It is to create the kind of home in which each member can feel comfortable, be nurtured and supported, and experience general well-being. Whatever you do that achieves such ends is important and is being true to God's calling. We believe that Paul's admonition to the church to do all things "decently and in order" (1 Corinthians 14:40) is as important for the home as it is for a congregation. A well-kept, orderly home, therefore, is a spiritual task. And fulfilling that task in a responsible way means that you are living out your love for one another. Now let's be realistic. Even defining the job of dishwashing as a spiritual task doesn't mean you're going to joyously whistle "Amazing Grace" every time you do it. But it will certainly help if you remind yourself that this task makes a contribution to the smooth running of your home and is not merely a chore.

What Can Someone Else Do?

The fact that maintaining a clean and orderly home is a spiritual task does not mean that you have to do it all. We suggested in the last chapter that you subcontract some household tasks, if possible and if necessary, to others. Note we say "some" and not "all," because it is important for you to do some of the tasks yourselves even if you can afford to pay others to do all of them. As we've said, investing some time and energy into caring for your home is a way of loving your family and fulfilling your calling.

If you have children, don't neglect to delegate some tasks to them. Even young children can contribute. In fact, they *should* begin to help and to get the sense at an early age that they have responsibilities to help the family function well. We recently watched a three-year-old girl set the table for a family dinner and beam with pride when her parents complimented her on the good job she had done.

What Can You Live With?

Whether you do all the work yourself or pay someone else to help, you may have a problem if family members have differing standards about what a decent and orderly house looks like. Adolescents have notoriously low standards. Many husbands and wives also differ. You may think of your spouse as messy, while he or she thinks of you as obsessively clean. In that case, it's time to follow a fundamental rule of a good marriage: Accept the acceptable. Don't insist on what you consider ideal. Rather, decide what you can live with. That is, find a middle ground where you both feel comfortable. Then, learn to live with the acceptable, because the way your house looks and the way tasks are done are not as important as the way your marriage works.

Two situations illustrate the point. The first involves our oldest son. When he was ten, we had a tiled basement floor that he and his siblings used for roller-skating. We assigned him the task of periodically cleaning the skate marks from the floor. At first, we agonized over what turned out to be a lengthy and frustrating process. We wanted the job done quickly. He worked slowly, but meticulously, using a steel wool scouring pad to obliterate every mark from the floor. The happy outcome was that we decided to let him do the work on his own schedule. We didn't get the job done as quickly as we would have preferred. On the other hand, we didn't have to do it ourselves, and the spotless floor was much more than we expected.

The other situation involves Chuck and Sally, a two-career couple who struggled over the division of labor in their home. One day Sally wrote down everything each of them was doing around the house. Chuck was dismayed when he saw the length of her list and the shortness of his. He volunteered to assume some of her tasks, including the grocery shopping. Sally was particularly delighted to turn the shopping over to him, because she hated running to the store. Her delight was temporarily dampened when she discovered that Chuck frequently came home with several items that were both expensive and, in her judgment, unnecessary. But she eventually put this in perspective:

> Chuck is an impulse buyer. He sees something that sounds exotic or tasty and buys it whether we ever eat that kind of food or not. So our grocery bill is higher since he's doing the shopping. But getting rid of the hassle and gaining some extra time is well worth the extra cost to me.

The point is, if you don't do the task yourself, it may not be done the way you would do it. The challenge is not how you can get your spouse to do the work your way or according to your standards, but rather to find what is acceptable for both of you. If it isn't done the way you would do it, can you live with it? If so, be quiet and be grateful you didn't have to do it yourself.

What Tasks Can You Exchange?

As Anne and Bill discovered, men and women don't have to do traditionally male and female tasks. What each of you does, and what your children do, should depend on what you each prefer—to the extent that is possible. Why shouldn't the wife take care of the car while the husband does laundry if that is what each of them prefers? And why not let children exchange tasks in accord with their preferences?

Household tasks are performed more efficiently and more effectively when family members are doing what they prefer. For example, Sally's initial dismay with Chuck's impulse buying was compounded when an older female neighbor said to her one day: "I saw Chuck at the grocery store. You're so lucky. There aren't many men who would shop for their wives." Her uneasiness with the higher grocery bills, combined with the notion that she might be neglecting one of her womanly duties while Chuck was doing something unmanly, nearly led her to take the job back from him. She thought about the matter carefully and decided against it:

> I decided that my neighbor's understanding of what men and women should or should not be doing was not going to be my guide. More important when I thought about taking that job back from Chuck, I realized how much I had always disliked the grocery shopping. But he really likes it!

On the other hand, Chuck dislikes yard work. So while he has taken over a number of tasks from Sally, she, in turn, has taken over one from him. She weeds and trims the lawn and garden—an ideal trade-off for them!

What Can You Do Together?

Household tasks are not necessarily something that you must finish before you can be together. Many chores can be done as a joint enterprise. For instance, some couples find it more enjoyable to clean the house and then work in the garden together, rather than one spouse working inside while the other works outside.

A physical therapist told us that one of her happiest childhood memories is of her family's weekly cleaning day. It was happy not because she enjoyed the tasks, but because of the way the work was done:

We worked as a family. Everyone had something to do. I can't remember a time when my parents didn't give my brothers and me some kind of chore on cleaning day. And when I was older, I remember working side by side with them as a team. We turned on the record player and listened to music as we worked. My father always picked upbeat music—I think he believed this made us work faster. And I can still see my mother and father doing things like vacuuming and dusting in time to the music. The more you do together as a couple or as a family, the more opportunities you have for building intimacy while getting necessary tasks done.

Take Time To . . .

1. Work together to develop a fresh mind-set about household chores. Concentrate on developing the idea that "this is *our* house, *our* yard, and *our* car." In other words, maintenance of these things is your joint responsibility. If you approach household chores this way, it will be much easier to find a fair way to share these responsibilities.

2. Find ways to increase your hours together by demanding less than perfection and finding acceptable compromises for completing tasks around the house.

3. Decide on some tasks that you can do together. For example, it's fun to share cooking dinner and cleaning up afterward. This gives you time to talk, to catch up on the events of the day, and to just enjoy being together.

4. Be with each other even if the work around the house isn't finished. It's important to remember that, no matter how efficient and fair and accepting you are, household chores can consume—if you let them—every waking moment you have at home together. Better to spend time with each other than with a greasy oven or a dirty car.

6

Building Intimacy When You Are Surrounded

"Therefore what God has joined together, let no one separate."
Matthew 19:6

"I thought our schedule was crazy before we had kids. Now I divide my life into b. c. and a. c.—before and after children. There's no comparison. When I hear childless couples complain about not having enough time together, I have to laugh. 'Just wait,' I warn them. 'You don't know what busy is until you have kids.'"
Kent—financial planner, husband, father of two

"I had always heard that you marry a family as well as a spouse, but I never realized the trouble this could cause. Ross's family makes demands on our time that really bother me. They don't seem to realize how important it is for us to have time alone together."
Mary Beth—book editor, recently married

---

*W*hat comes to mind when you hear Jesus' words: "What God has joined together, let no one separate"? Put differently, what kinds of things can tear apart a marriage? Or to personalize the matter, what would you include on a list of challenges and threats to your marriage? Would children be on your list? Relatives? Friends? We usually think of children, family, and friends as part of the glue that holds marriages together. And they can be. They can also be difficult and stressful. Even at their best, they can add to the many demands on your time. How, then, do you deal with these important relationships in ways that strengthen rather than diminish your marital intimacy?

Can Parents Be Partners?

Kent laughs when his childless friends talk about time pressure. He knows how consuming children can be. He also knows that marital intimacy can be blindsided by the "blessed event." It nearly happened to him:

> Cara and I were thrilled when she got pregnant with our first child. The pregnancy went well, and the birth wasn't too difficult. But when our son was a few months old, I began to have an uneasy feeling about our marriage. We seemed to be drifting apart. It's like we were living together but not really connected.

What happened to Cara and Kent after the baby came? Although both were excited about being parents, Kent soon that like he was a distant second in Cara's life. They had been married for five years before Cara got pregnant and had enjoyed the intimacy of being alone together. Kent particularly valued the way in which Cara made him feel special in her life.

Now he had to share Cara with a third person. As Kent saw it, spontaneity and, for the most part, sex, had disappeared from their lives. And when they talked, conversations focused primarily on the baby. Kent felt that something very meaningful had vanished from his life.

In essence, Kent and Cara had discovered in an unsettling way what all new parents face: A baby dramatically changes your life. Children are a blessing, but they are also a challenge in your continuing effort to build marital intimacy. Moreover, as Cara points out, the challenge becomes more severe as the size of your family increases:

> It was a lot easier when we had just one child. One of us could do household chores while the other took care of the baby. Afterward, Kent and I had time together. Now we each take care of the children and then do a few household chores before we fall into bed exhausted.

Fortunately, Cara and Kent have found ways to nurture their relationship in spite of the time demands of parenting. Guarding their calendar is crucial to the task. They try to schedule times together a month in advance, and also try to find additional, more spontaneous moments during the week. For instance, they both work in downtown offices and so they often lunch together. "I never thought that just having a fast-food hamburger with Cara would be so special," Kent notes. "But when you're as busy as we are, it's *very* special."

Of course your children also have needs, and you don't want to underestimate those needs. Neither do you want to overestimate them. As you plan your calendar, therefore, it is important to be realistic about the needs of your children.

What Children Need—And Don't Need

Don't get caught in the trap of thinking that your children's needs are met as long as you spend a certain amount of time with them. Children do require time, of course. But the only way to maintain time for your marriage is to *focus on their needs rather than on how many minutes or hours you spend with them.* There are times when they will require more of you and other times when they will require less. The important thing is to be sensitive to whether they are getting what they need from you.

What is it that children need from you? In brief, they need to

- feel that they are wanted;
- believe that they are important in your life;
- feel secure about being cared for and protected by you;
- hear words of praise from you;
- have their lives structured by rules and know that the rules will be enforced;
- have the freedom to explore their world and to discover their own unique gifts and inclinations;
- learn how to be socially adept, that is, learn what is acceptable and unacceptable so that they can relate well to others;
- get a growing sense of the enormity of God's love for them, a sense that develops as they experience *your* love for them.

You have a major role in meeting each of the above needs. While you will fulfill them in differing ways as your children grow, the needs exist at every age.

The question, then, is not How many minutes will you allocate to your child today? Instead, the question is, What will you do to help your child feel wanted and important? What words of praise can you offer? As long as the children's needs are being cared for, you need not feel constrained to spend all of your free moments with them.

You've probably heard of the notion that "quality time" is what really matters. It's true, but what is quality time? It isn't necessarily participating in a special event. We've seen parents on outings at the zoo, beach, or amusement park whose thoughts are clearly on other matters. Their whole demeanor cries out that they are only partly with their children. Quality time occurs when you are fully engaged with your children, not merely when you are doing something special with them.

Keeping in mind that you must be fully engaged, here are a few suggestions on ways to have quality time with your children:

- Give your child some special time every day when you really connect with each other. In the Lauer family, our three kids usually gathered in the middle of our bed each night before they went to sleep. We'd talk about the good, and the not-so-good, things that had happened during that day and about their plans for the next day. Our discussions covered every imaginable topic and, as they grew older, some that we hadn't even imagined.
- Pray with your child regularly at mealtimes and before bedtime.
- End every day with a moment of affirmation, verbalizing your love and praising your child in some way.
- Relate your experiences of growing up. Your child will delight in knowing what kind of boy or girl you were and about your successes and struggles.
- Talk to your child about your work. Tell about the tedious and frustrating aspects as well as the exciting and fulfilling things you do.
- Make it a general rule to have dinner together as a family. The ritual of enjoyable family meals can be one of your child's more rewarding experiences.

Notice something about the above items? None of them consumes huge amounts of time. You will want to plan special things with your child, of course. But the times that will be cherished the most are those when he or she simply connected with you. A mother discovered this when her plans were interrupted by rain:

> I had always thought that my parents were too busy to do much with me when I was growing up and didn't want to make the same mistake with my daughter. So I went to the other extreme. I continually planned some special event for her. We went to the zoo, the children's museum, the playground, and to every children's attraction that came to town.
>
> One Saturday we planned to go to the park, but it rained hard all day. So we just stayed at home. We made cookies, played games, talked, and read together. When my daughter said her nightly prayers, she thanked God for the "bestest" day she had ever had.

For the first time, the mother realized what her daughter really needed—not to be constantly with her or continually entertained by her, but to connect with her and share with her as parent and child.

As the mother discovered, a good part of effectively meeting the needs of your children is to be aware of what they *don't* need from you. Some of those things are obvious. They don't need to feel neglected or unwanted or belittled or inferior. But they also don't need to be overly indulged or have everything done for them so that they have no opportunities to learn how to be independent. Your children don't need to be so protected and so cared for that they have difficulty fending for themselves in the world outside the home.

The point is, you are called to be your children's parent, not their God. Whether from guilt or from desire, don't fall into the trap of giving yourself so completely to your children that you have no time for your marriage. In fact, we would add an item to the above list of your children's needs: to experience the richness of a home with parents who have a happy and secure marriage.

Your Marriage: A Priceless Gift to Your Children

Everyone who has grown up in a troubled or broken home, and every counselor who has dealt with the human wreckage resulting from unhappy and broken homes, knows the value for children of living in a home with parents who have a solid marriage. If your marriage is stable and satisfying, you give invaluable help to your children in two ways. You provide the best possible context for their healthy development, and you provide a model for their own future intimate relationships.

Even if you're convinced of the benefits for your children, how do you build this kind of marriage when the kids consume so much of your time? In addition to the things we have already mentioned, we suggest you also try the following:

1. *Talk with other couples in similar situations about ways they build marital intimacy.* Some of them will probably be frustrated and perplexed, but some will have ideas you can use. For example, our discussions with other couples have yielded such ideas as the following:

- Get help from other friends, neighbors, or grandparents. You can trade off baby-sitting time with friends and neighbors. And grandparents—if you are considerate of their schedule— usually are thrilled to sit for a few hours. A father of three preschool children told us that one way he and his wife get some time together is to take the kids to their grandparents. Then they slip out for a couple of hours and have dinner, take a walk, or do something that gives them a chance to connect with each other.

When they get back, "the kids hardly know we've been gone." Parents, grandparents, and children all benefited!

- Get up early and have coffee together before the children awake.
- One evening a week, feed the kids first, then have your own candlelight dinner after they go to bed.

2. *Use the problem-solving technique discussed in chapter three.* In this case, the problem is: How can we find time for each other? You may be surprised to find out how many ideas you can come up with when you use your own creative imagination.

3. *Be willing to give up something.* Recall your first decision—to give priority to your relationship. When a couple say to us, "No matter how hard we try, we can't think of ways to find time for each other in our busy schedules," our response is, "Then what can you give up to make time?"

Of course, there may be times when your schedules won't allow you to have the intimate experiences you want and need. But a chronic lack of time for each other means you have a desperate need to look at your life and decide what you will give up. As a busy husband and father realized:

When Becky and I didn't take time for each other, our children suffered, too. The problems in our relationship affected the way we dealt with them. We finally realized that we could only be good parents if we were good marriage partners. And we realized that we couldn't have a good marriage unless we cut something out of our schedules. So Becky agreed to give up a quilting group she met with every week, and I agreed to give up playing tennis on Saturday mornings. At

first, we each felt deprived of something important to us. But the gain for our marriage and our
family now makes what we gave up seem trivial
by comparison.

Then There's Those Other People

Children are not the only challenge to your time.
Extended family and friends can also pose a problem. Mary
Beth has been married less than a year, but already feels
the intrusion of Ross's family in her marriage:

> The only real problem Ross and I have is his fam-
> ily. Well, Ross is part of the problem, too,
> because he won't stand up to them. If his mother
> calls and says she needs something from him, he
> can't say no to her—even when we've already
> planned something for the two of us.
> One weekend, we were going away on a short
> trip so we could have some uninterrupted time
> together. Guess what? Ross's brother called to
> tell us he was coming to town for the weekend
> and would like to stay at our house. I said that
> was fine, he could use the house while we were
> gone. But Ross thought that would be insulting
> to his brother, who expected us to stay at home
> and entertain him.

Clearly, Ross is struggling with the conflicting demands
of marriage and family. He must learn to help his family
understand that Mary Beth is his primary commitment
while, at the same time, affirming his love for them.

Although most families are not as exacting as Ross's,
most couples have a long list of people who make
demands on their time: his family, her family, friends,
work colleagues, professional organizations, the church,
the PTA, Little League, and so on. And just when you

think you have a few minutes of privacy on a quiet Sunday afternoon, the doorbell rings and someone wants to talk with you about a local bond issue or political campaign.

The claims on our time are numberless. In most cases, the claims are from good and worthy people or groups, which makes them harder to resist. It's always difficult to turn down a request to teach Sunday school, or be the local representative for the United Way, or go with friends on a picnic. Nevertheless, there are times when you just have to say no, even to some very worthwhile endeavors. To assist you in handling the demands of your extended families, friends, church, and community, we offer The Ten Commandments of Relationships for Busy Couples:

1. *Remember thy marriage, to keep it holy.* This first commandment reminds you again that your relationship with your spouse, second only to your relationship with God, is your primary commitment. It is no accident that Paul used the analogy of Christ and the church to discuss the relationship of a husband and wife (Ephesians 5:25-33). The marital relationship is similar to that between Christ and his church—it is holy, a sacred trust, and must be protected from anything intrusive. The other nine commandments must be lived out with this one as a guiding principle.

2. *Honor thy extended family, and accept its love, support, and assistance.* We have already noted that the extended family can put a strain on marriage. Those, like Ross, who feel compelled to accede to every demand and expectation honor neither their extended families nor their marriages. But the extended family can also be an important source of support. It can provide invaluable help, including emotional support, baby-sitting, advice when it is solicited, companionship, and even financial assistance. Some young couples are loathe to accept financial help from family. However, if the help is offered without strings, as an expression of love and concern, it should be accepted with gratitude. To do so is to honor your extended family.

3. *Thou shalt practice Christian assertiveness.* If you have not had an assertiveness training class, or are not sure what it means to be assertive, we recommend that you read a good book on the topic, preferably one that talks about assertiveness as a Christian trait. In essence, we define Christian assertiveness as openly and honestly working for fairness in human relationships. A biblical example is found in Acts 16. Paul and Silas were flogged and jailed without just cause in Philippi. The next morning, the magistrates who ordered the punishment sent word to free them. What would a Christian response be? To go quietly away and forget the incident? Paul did no such thing:

> But Paul replied, "They have beaten us in public, uncondemned, men who are Roman citizens, and have thrown us into prison; and now are they going to discharge us in secret? Certainly not! Let them come and take us out themselves." (Acts 16:37)

The magistrates apologized for their behavior. In the process, they learned that they could not act unjustly with impunity. Christian assertiveness does not mean to get your own way, but to be open and honest about what is fair so that everyone is treated properly.

Ross could use some Christian assertiveness in dealing with his family. In the long run, everyone would benefit. If you are not assertive in face of the horde of demands on you, your life will be run by others and your marriage will always be threatened.

4. *Thou shalt not commit emotional adultery.* Who is your best friend? If the answer is not your spouse, you may be guilty of emotional adultery. For your primary—note, please, we say your primary and not your sole—source of emotional support should be your spouse. Marriages get into trouble when one or both partners invest most of

their emotional energy in a friend or colleague. And if the friend or colleague is of the opposite sex, the chances for marital problems increase dramatically.

Even if emotional adultery doesn't lead to physical adultery, the results can be devastating for a marriage. A tearful wife talked to us about her husband's "affair" and how it had ruined their marriage. It turned out that she had no evidence that physical adultery had ever occurred, and she acknowledged that her husband firmly insisted that it had not. But this did not ease her feelings of betrayal: "Even if he wasn't sexually involved, he treated her like a wife and me like a stranger."

5. *Thou shalt not steal time from thy spouse and spend it on community involvement.* We believe that Christians need to be involved in their communities. How else can you be salt to the earth or a light in the world? The issue is not whether to be involved, but how much to be involved. As a couple, you need to decide such issues as how many community organizations you can belong to, and whether you should belong only to those where you can both participate. The community is important, but you must not steal time from your partner to serve the community.

6. *Thou shalt learn to say no with firm confidence.* You can learn this as you practice Christian assertiveness. We say "firm confidence" because if you waffle when you turn down a request you are fair game for some arm-twisting efforts. "No" is appropriate at church as well as other situations. We have known some Christians who feel guilty if they turn down any request to serve at their church. But whether the church or any other group, if saying yes to the organization means saying no to needs of your marriage, your responsibility is clear. Remember Commandment One.

7. *Thou shalt not covet others' approval to the detriment of thy marriage.* Some people have a problem saying no because they need the approval of those who ask. Ross

needs to maintain the approval of family members and that's why he won't say no to them. Many people need the approval of people in high places—their boss, their pastor, their doctor. You may have similar needs. If you didn't get much praise as a child, you may generally have a strong need for approval from everyone. If so, keep in mind an important fact: When you exercise Christian assertiveness, you will usually gain the respect—and thereby, the approval—of others. And if you don't get their approval, it's okay. You'll gain a more important approval—that of your spouse and your God.

8. *Thou shalt not kill equity by leaving thy spouse out of thy decision making.* In deciding about your involvement with family, friends, and community, be certain that all decisions are joint ones. It is one thing to agree together that you will each participate in no more than two community organizations, and quite another to announce arbitrarily that you are limiting yourself to two groups. Equity is priceless. Guard it well.

9. *Thou shalt not put personal pleasure before thy spouse.* Some of the requests that come to you will involve things you like to do. Many parents thoroughly enjoy being the coach of a child's soccer team. Many people love involvement in political organizations or cultural events. In other words, you may be reluctant to say no because of the personal pleasure involved. There's nothing wrong with that. Again, just remember your primary commitment.

10. *Thou shalt love thy neighbor as thyself.* This is to remind you not to carry some of the above ideas to an extreme. We know a few couples, even very busy couples, who become too focused on themselves. They live for their own pleasure and give little thought to children, family, or community. The point is not to make your marriage an idol, but to protect and nurture your marriage in the face of more demands than any human can meet.

Take Time To . . .

1. Establish your own traditions as a couple. This will strengthen your primary commitment to each other and confirm that you constitute a separate entity from your extended families. For example, spouses often struggle with the expectations of both of their families concerning how and where to spend holidays or other special occasions. One way to change these expectations is gradually to create and observe your own traditions. When appropriate, invite extended family members to share in these events with you.

2. Cultivate close and vital connections with your children. That is, work on really being with them when you are together. This is the most effective way to use your time and is guaranteed to produce the best results.

3. Commit to making dinner together a family ritual. If you have children, feed the kids early one evening a week—or once every two weeks, or once a month—enjoy their conversation, and then have a candlelight dinner for the two of you. The cuisine doesn't have to be fancy; pizza or carry-out Chinese will do fine. The point is to have a few moments together even though you're surrounded.

4. Participate in a community organization that you can enjoy together. It may be singing in the choir, playing on a coed softball team, joining a book discussion group, or sponsoring a couples' enrichment group. The possibilities are endless and the benefits are great. You will enlarge your common interests, make a contribution to the community, and increase your time together.

7

Taking Care of Yourself: A Gift for Your Spouse

"Or do you not know that your body is a temple of the Holy Spirit within you, which you have from God, and that you are not your own?"

1 Corinthians 6:19

> *"I have been running now for three years, and I love it. I run for about forty-five minutes five days a week, and it makes me feel great. But my running is causing problems with my husband, Dick. He accuses me of being self-indulgent, spending this amount of time each week on myself. Sometimes he makes me feel guilty. But not enough to make me give up my running."*
>
> Diana—wife, librarian, mother
>
> *"We've been happily married for more than fifteen years. And I believe that one of the main reasons our marriage has lasted is that Lorna is more interesting to me now than when we were first married. She is more interesting as a wife, more interesting as a woman, more interesting as a sexual partner, and more interesting as a friend."*
>
> Greg—police captain, husband, father

How many different people do you expect to be married to during your lifetime? Before you answer, or think that you know the answer we would like to hear, listen to the account of a man who has been married for twenty-seven years:

85

I've been married to a succession of different women, but I've only had one wife. She keeps growing as a person, and it's been my privilege to share in her growth. Like every couple, we've had our ups and downs. Over the years, she has thrilled me, surprised me, frustrated me, and angered me. But I have to say, she has never bored me.

If variety is the spice of life, the good news is that you can have it with your present partner. While giving each other the stability of your commitment, you can also give each other the stimulation of your growth. Just as a good marriage is a blessed gift to your children, so your well-being—taking care of yourself—is a blessed gift to your spouse. Exactly what does it mean to take care of yourself, and how do you fit this into your busy schedule?

Keep Growing

One part of self-care is personal development—an essential for a fulfilling life and for the well-being of your marriage. Those in long-term satisfying marriages report that their spouses grow more interesting to them as the years go by. And spouses grow more interesting as they expand their interests and develop their skills. Thus, Greg explained why his wife, Lorna, has become a more interesting person over the course of their fifteen-year marriage:

She's a very curious person. She's always eager to learn something new. And that includes new ways of dealing with people, new ways to shape our relationship, and new information about everything you can think of from science to sports. If one of our children wants to pursue a new hobby, Lorna gets enthused and involved. In some ways, she's like a kid herself—fascinated by the world she lives in and always wanting to understand things better.

You need not have the widespread range of interests of someone like Lorna to keep growing. But you do need to continue developing your interests and abilities. You need to become more competent in dealing with people. You need to develop your faith, to "grow up in every way into him who is the head, into Christ" (Ephesians 4:15). In essence, then, to be a growing individual means that you are increasingly able to

- relate warmly and intimately with others;
- accept yourself, including both your potential and your limitations;
- take responsibility for your own behavior;
- have a realistic and expanding understanding of your world;
- acknowledge and express your feelings;
- shape your behavior and thoughts in accordance with a commitment to Jesus Christ.

Some of the activities or projects that can help you achieve the above are

- reading (be certain to include books and articles with views different from your own);
- investigating, on a regular basis, something about which you know little or nothing (it can be anything from the political situation in the Middle East to how an internal combustion engine works to diverse theological perspectives);
- changing your hair or clothing style, your home furnishings, or your typical way of greeting people;
- developing the habit of going beyond chitchat

by talking with people about their work, their interests, their families;
- planning to do something new with your spouse every few months or so;
- cultivating a new friendship;
- acquiring a new skill—mechanical, artistic, or interpersonal;
- learning more about an interest of your spouse or about your spouse's line of work;
- volunteering to help in one of your church's outreach programs, such as visiting an orphanage, housing and feeding the homeless, or working at a hospital;
- developing a more meaningful prayer life by trying various forms of prayer (ask your pastor for books and other help).

Some of the above may require more time than you have available at present. But you may be able to substitute some of them for something else currently in your life, and some—like engaging in more than chitchat—may require no additional time at all. The point is, whatever you do to grow as a person will make you a more fulfilled (and more fascinating) individual and will add spice to your marriage.

Guard Your Temple

It is rather awesome to think that "your body is a temple of the Holy Spirit within you" (1 Corinthians 6:19). We believe this has serious implications for the way we take care of ourselves physically. If we abuse our bodies with such things as stress, smoking, drinking, and overeating, we are treating God's temple shabbily.

There is a glut of information about maintaining a healthy body. Let's just review three things that are important and doable for busy people:

Learn to Relax

Just as a rutted and rocky road beats up a car, stress beats up your body. We don't know any way to *avoid* stress. But there are ways to *deal* with it and minimize its effects, all of which involve learning how to relax and ease the tension out of your body. Most of us know intuitively that from time to time we have to relax—that's why many people resort to smoking or drinking or long sessions in front of the TV. But there are more effective, more time-efficient, and healthier ways to relax. Try one or more of the following.

1. *Deep, abdominal breathing.* Breathe deeply, filling your lungs completely, and then slowly exhale. Repeat the process several times. As you do this, imagine relaxation coming into your body and the tension going out. Practice this frequently during the day, especially when you feel the tension mounting.

2. *Progressive relaxation.* In progressive relaxation, you alternately tense and relax muscles throughout the body. Begin at one extremity, such as your toes or head, and work through the rest of your body. To see the effects, tense your neck muscles for a few seconds, then release and relax them as much as possible. Repeat a couple of times and note how you feel. You can find books that will give you more details and help you to perfect this method.

3. *The calculated slowdown.* The busier people are, the faster they seem to run, and the more tense they become. We know, because it happens to us all the time. The calculated slowdown is one way we break the "hurry cycle." When we find ourselves rushing from one task or one place to another, we deliberately slow down. For example, we drive more slowly on the freeway or walk more leisurely down the supermarket isles. This isn't as easy as it sounds, but the benefits are real. Physically and mentally you slow down to match your more leisurely pace.

An important point about relaxation is that you must

find what works for you. You may be one of those people who can relax by lying spread-eagled on your bed and thinking of your body as an empty potato sack. If it works for you, do it.

Exercise

Exercise does a number of things for you. When you are under stress, your body automatically goes into what psychologists call the fight or flight mode of response. This response involves, among other things, an increased flow of adrenaline, higher blood pressure, and a slowing down of your digestive system. Exercise helps burn up the hormones produced as a result of this response. It lowers your adrenaline, reduces your blood pressure, and improves your digestion. Exercise also builds stamina, cleans out your blood vessels, takes your mind off stressors, and creates natural relaxers (more endorphins and sounder sleep).

You should always consult a physician before embarking on a vigorous exercise program. But your program doesn't need to be elaborate or exhausting. Vigorous walking, done on a regular basis, may be all the exercise you require. You need not be like the man who appeared at work after a hard morning's exercising and moaned: "I feel like I'm killing myself in order to stay healthy."

Nor is it necessary for exercise to consume large chunks of your scarce time. There are a lot of ways you can incorporate exercise into your regular activities: Take the stairs instead of the elevator; park your car farther away from your destination; take a walk rather than a sit-down coffee break; exercise during part of your lunch hour; or walk the dog farther, faster, or more often than you do now.

Practice Good Eating Habits

Some people handle stress by eating themselves to death. Others lose their appetites and increase their stress by poor nutrition. Good nutrition can help you handle the stresses of life, so pay attention to those things that we know are good for you: emphasize high-fiber foods; reduce your intake of fat, sugar, caffeine, and salt; drink lots of water; and stop eating before you feel full.

You're Not Selfish; You're Desirable

Dick unsettled his wife, Diana, who thought she was improving both herself and her marriage by her running, when he told her she was being selfish. We encouraged Diana to continue running and to help Dick see it in a different light. Those who keep themselves as healthy as possible are not only protecting God's temple but are sending a message of affirmation and commitment to their spouses. "You're not selfish," we told her, "you're keeping yourself healthy. And that's a compliment and a gift to your husband."

Protect and Nurture Your Emotions

Taking care of your body demands that you also take care of your emotions. Physical and emotional problems feed on and nurture each other. For instance, have you ever dealt with someone who was literally a "pain in the neck," that is, someone who upset you so much that you developed physical symptoms? Most of us have. On the other hand, people with severe physical ailments tend to find their emotions affected—they struggle with frustration, anger, and depression. You can't segregate your physical and emotional states.

Busy people often neglect their emotional health. They are oblivious to the emotional toll that results from pushing themselves too hard and too long. The following suggestions, therefore, provide ways to safeguard your emotions from the stresses of your hurried life and to build positive mental health.

Take Responsibility for Yourself

We all have to deal with situations that are less than ideal. Your boss is generally tyrannical, your spouse is often exasperating, your children are frequently frustrating, and your in-laws are always impossible. So what do you do? Do you wait for "something" to happen, or "someone" to come and rescue you? This is precisely what many people do.

A first step in dealing with stress and a fundamental step in being an emotionally healthy individual is to take responsibility for yourself. This means that *you* take some kind of action that will enable you to cope with the situation. Your boss may be tyrannical, but you are responsible for how you respond to him or her. Your marriage may be having difficulties, but you are as responsible as your spouse for addressing the problems. And so on. The point is, don't play the victim game—the game of if-only: "My life would be okay if only you . . . or if only he . . . or if only she . . . ."

Jesus emphasized the importance of being personally responsible in the parable of the talents (Matthew 25: 14-30). The master entrusted money to each of three servants before he went on a journey. Only the two who used the money responsibly were rewarded. The fearful one, who fretted and anxiously hid the money entrusted to him, lost everything.

Use Visualization

Visualization is a technique of taking a stressful or problematic situation and dealing with it positively in your imagination. At worst, it saves you from sitting around and imagining all kinds of dire outcomes. At best, it enables you to deal with the situation in a healthy way.

Here is how it works. Take a situation or person that is troublesome in some way. Sit down and get yourself into a relaxed state. Then imagine the person, activity, or situation as realistically and vividly as you can. Imagine Christ with you, helping you to deal with the matter. Practice this until you feel relaxed about the problem.

For instance, suppose that you're stressed by the expectations of a family member. You know that you need to be assertive and confront the person, but the thought terrifies you. Find a place where you can relax. Then close your eyes and imagine as vividly as you can and, in as much detail as possible, the way you will approach the person. Be sure to imagine Christ with you, supporting and guiding you. For as long as Christ is with you, you can live with whatever outcome occurs.

Affirm Your Own Worth

Life in the fast lane can be harmful to your sense of personal worth. A steady diet of time-pressured days and too many crises can leave you feeling vulnerable, inept, and helpless—rather like the man who insisted that his marital problems were his fault, even though he wasn't sure exactly why his wife was upset or what he could do to repair the damage. To affirm your own worth means to have self-respect. A sense of personal worth is necessary for emotional health. It is also essential to a healthy marriage; no relationship can thrive when one of the partners generally feels unworthy. And if you doubt that, just think about the kind of people you like to be around. It's unlikely that any of them battle constantly with feelings of worthlessness.

One way to affirm your worth is to remind yourself continually of a fundamental doctrine of the Christian faith— God loves you so much that he gave his only Son for you. And what God loves is never worthless.

Learn the Art of Reframing

Reframing means simply that you develop a new perspective. It is based on the fact that there are always different ways of looking at any situation. If you look at a situation in one way, you can cause yourself a good deal of mental anguish; looked at in another way, you can deal with the situation with equanimity.

For instance, how would you look upon being unjustly put into jail? When this happened to Paul and Silas (Acts 16:16-28), they could have railed angrily against a system that allowed such injustice to occur. Instead, they looked on it as an opportunity to witness to their faith. Similarly, James (1:2) tells us to "consider it nothing but joy" when we meet various trials, because the testing of our faith produces steadfastness and that will make us more perfect Christians. So instead of thinking about the burden of the trials, he says, think about the ultimate, gratifying outcome.

As James points out, we can always reframe because virtually every situation has a mix of positive and negative elements. So the question is, What do you focus on? It's the old thing about whether the cup is half empty or half full. But it works. When Greg and Lorna were married, he hoped she would always "stay just the way you are." It was a little disquieting to him when she began to change. At first, he resisted. Then he reframed the change, viewing it as not only a normal but a stimulating process of growth that could enrich their relationship. Today, he celebrates his changing wife.

Affirm Your Control

A study of business executives found that some seemed to function well under the same amount of stress that made others sick. The researchers concluded that one important reason was that those who continued to function well knew that they always had some degree of control over their lives.

We can't control our lives completely. "I am the master of my fate" is nonsense. But you always have some control. You are never powerless. Otherwise, taking responsibility for yourself would be meaningless.

It is important to remind yourself that you have some control, and to exercise that control. Reframing is a way of exercising your control when you face a troublesome situation; you control the way you think about the situation. Confrontation is a way of exercising your control when you're stressed by some individual. Pruning some activities out of your schedule is a way of exercising control when you're overloaded.

The point is, you always have options. And one option, depending on the circumstances, may be to do nothing. Don't get trapped into thinking that if you don't complete a task, the world will collapse. Ask yourself "what if" questions. What if the house doesn't get cleaned today? What will happen? What if I say no to that request? What will happen? Frequently, we just plod ahead and do things that are stressful without ever questioning what would happen if we didn't do them, or if we did them at a later time, or if we enlisted someone else's help in doing them.

Heather took control when her marriage seemed in a rut. Her husband was spending long hours at work. They seldom went out together. She wanted to attend a marriage enrichment weekend, but her husband insisted he couldn't spare the time. She urged him to read a book about marriage with her, but he was always too tired. She began to feel hopeless and helpless. She went to a counselor, who reminded her that she still had one option—she could change something about herself or her behavior. One evening she dressed up, told her husband she was going to a movie, and left the house before he could fashion words of protest. She had asked him to take her to see this movie on several occasions, and each time he had refused. She told us: "I really felt strange going by myself, but I really wanted to see the movie. And I also hoped to get my husband's attention." When she got home, her husband apologized for not going along and promised to spend more time with her. Heather reports that her husband is sometimes dismayed by her newfound independence, but he is also intrigued. It has given their marriage a needed shot of vitality.

Cultivate Your Sense of Humor

Don't neglect to laugh. Most situations have a humorous side; look for them. Develop a repertoire of funny stories. Encourage people to tell you jokes. Save particularly funny cartoons and hang them on your refrigerator. In other words, cultivate laughter and make it a part of your daily life, because laughter is soul medicine. And when you share it with your spouse, it becomes couple medicine.

Double Your Pleasure—Do It Together

Self-development can be both an individual and a couple exercise. There are some things you may *need* to do as an individual. Diana, for instance, must necessarily run without Dick because he has knee problems that prevent his participation. There are some things you *should* do as an individual. The point of self-development is not to make you clones but rather to make you intriguing to each other.

On the other hand, because your schedules do not permit you the luxury of a lot of alone time, at least some of your self-development can occur together. For many years, we have exercised together and have found it an excellent time to discuss our plans for the day, talk over any concerns, and share ideas—all the while taking our minds off of the pain of exercising. Thus, we gain both as individuals and as a couple. The exercise keeps each of us fit, and the talk enriches us both personally and as a couple.

It's so easy for busy people to neglect themselves. There are so many important demands upon your time, so many people who want a piece of you. But it's absolutely essential that you take time for yourself—for your own physical, intellectual, emotional, and spiritual development. In the long run, it will be time well spent both for you personally and for your marriage.

Take Time To . . .

1. Take a walk today. You may only have time for a fifteen-minute stroll, but seize the opportunity. As you walk, engage with your surroundings; note the brisk breeze, the warmth of the sun, or the clarity of the nighttime sky. And communicate; use these rare moments to talk to yourself, to your spouse if he or she accompanies you, and to God who walks along with you.

2. Make driving a more beneficial necessity. Instead of racing to and from work or to some other required meeting, deliberately slow your speed and use the time to think and to pray. If you have a long commute, listen to books-on-tape during part of the drive. Whoever thought that driving could actually be good for your health!

3. Brush up on an old, or develop a new, intellectual interest. The possibilities are endless—anything from art to zoology will do. Even if you can only spend thirty minutes a week pursuing this interest, you will expand your horizons and, at the same time, make yourself a more fascinating person for your spouse.

8

The Long and Short of Intimate Talk

"O my dove, in the clefts of the rock,
  in the covert of the cliff,
let me see your face,
  let me hear your voice;
for your voice is sweet,
  and your face is lovely."
Song of Solomon 2:14

"I know I need to listen better, but it's really tough sometimes. Especially when Maggie goes on for fifteen minutes about something that isn't even important."
Shawn—husband, computer salesman

"Dean and I kept a record of our conversations for a week a few years ago. It was an assignment in our couples' group. And we were really shocked by the results. We found that we barely spoke to each other during the week and crammed most of our conversations into the weekends. Now we schedule a time for ourselves every day. It sounds strange to schedule a time to talk with your husband; but if we don't, it just doesn't happen."
Terry—wife, food service manager, mother

*H*ow much time did you spend talking with your spouse last week? Keep a log of your conversations for a week. Track the minutes and the topics. The results may surprise or even shock you. Like Terry and her husband, you may decide that you need to fit more intimate talk into your schedule. Because trying to build or even maintain intimacy without talking together is like trying to grow flowers without planting any seeds. It just won't happen.

The following conversation took place between a husband and wife who are struggling in their marriage:

> He: I need to be intimate with you. But you're shutting me out of your life. We never make love anymore.

> She: I need to be intimate with you, too. But it doesn't happen because you don't talk to me. I need you to share what you are thinking and feeling with me. I can't feel like making love with you when we never connect.

> He: But when are we going to talk? I'm not a morning person. And by the time the kids are in bed, you say you're too tired.

> She: If you were really willing to talk with me, I would find the time somehow.

This discussion underscores two points. First, the lack of conversation kills intimacy. And second, a lot of couples are so busy that they have difficulty finding the necessary time to talk together.

The Song of Solomon proclaims the importance of talking together when it says "for your voice is sweet, and your face is lovely" (Song of Solomon 2:14). These are not two unrelated matters. In the process of speaking to your spouse, you become more attractive to him or her. And lest anyone should chuckle at such a statement, we are aware that its validity depends on what your partner says and how he or she says it. Words have the capacity to destroy, but they also have the power to create and build. But the words must be uttered. It won't do to be like the man who confessed that he had given his wife "thousands of unspoken compliments." Compliments, along with other things, have to be articulated. Let's see how this can be accomplished in the midst of your busy life.

How Much Do You Talk?

It can be instructive and useful for you to log a week of your conversations to see how much time you talk and what you talk about. There's no single "right" amount of time; it depends on your needs. If you are not talking together at least a few hours each week, however, you probably need to copy the practice of Terry and Dean and schedule some conversation times. As Terry notes, if you have children, you may also have to alter their schedules:

> We used to let our kids stay up pretty late—until we went to bed. Now we get them into bed by eight. Then we go to our "couple's place," a love seat in the corner of our bedroom. We cuddle, relax, and talk about the day. We might spend just fifteen minutes, but it's a very important time for our marriage. For us, this time together has become almost sacred.

The point is to schedule time not just to *be* together, but to *talk* together. It could even be a time when you are doing something else—driving to church or to the store, cleaning up after dinner, or exercising. It isn't that you always have to be talking when you are together, but that you need a certain amount of time when you verbally connect with each other. And if the only time available is while you are doing something else, use it.

We recommend that you also schedule time for longer

conversations on your calendar. In fact, you might want to use your weekly calendar-planning session as a time to review the past week, sort out any problems that have developed, and discuss what you anticipate for the week ahead. Or you might schedule a weekly date where you avoid any mention of problems and concentrate on fun and romance. Talk about the things that you find attractive about your spouse, share your hopes and dreams, discuss your favorite romantic movie or book, and so forth. Even if you are currently struggling with a problem in your marriage, it can be very therapeutic to call a time-out and do something together that is strictly relaxing and fun.

What Do You Talk About?

When we were growing up, one of the favorite topics of teenage advice columns was how to keep a conversation going when you were on a date. The advice was generally aimed at females who were given the responsibility for avoiding awkward, embarrassing silences and encouraging their date to talk about himself. Getting your date to talk, we were told, was essential if you wanted to learn about him and build a future relationship.

Of course, keeping the conversation going is not the sole responsibility of either sex. But based on our observations of married couples dining out in restaurants, we wonder if anyone is taking responsibility these days for keeping the conversation going. You know what we're talking about— two married people (judging from the rings on their fingers) sitting together, not looking at, and only uttering an occasional word to, each other. Again, we're not saying that couples have to be talking the entire time they're together. They do need, however, to link up with each other in meaningful conversation regularly. Let's think, therefore, about what constitutes "meaningful" conversation.

Small Talk Is Necessary

When Shawn complained about having to listen to Maggie talk for fifteen minutes about an unimportant topic, we reminded him of two things. First, if Maggie wanted to talk about something for that length of time, it wasn't unimportant to her. And second, small talk, talk about relatively trivial rather than momentous matters, is important for marital health.

"Small talk" is probably an unfortunate term, because talking about day-to-day events with each other is far from trivial in terms of its impact on your intimacy. Unless the small talk is an attempt to avoid more serious issues, to converse with each other at a relatively trivial level is to connect and, thus, to build intimacy.

Occasionally we find someone like Shawn who not only doesn't want to listen to his spouse talk about things in which he isn't interested but also doesn't want to "burden" his spouse with matters outside their relationship. So for most of the time they've been married, Shawn has avoided talking about his work with Maggie. He feels that he is doing her a favor and helping his marriage by his silence.

Maggie feels differently about the matter:

> I need for Shawn to tell me about his work. He doesn't only have to talk about problems. I'd like to know some of the things he does while he's there. But I'd like to share the problems with him, too. I feel like he has a whole life that I'm shut out of, and that really troubles me.

We have reminded Shawn a number of times that sharing his workday with Maggie is a way of integrating their lives, a way of becoming one flesh, a way of having intertwined rather than parallel lives.

Shawn has taken our advice and started talking about

his work with Maggie. As a result, they both feel a deeper intimacy in their marriage, a fact that surprised Shawn:

> I couldn't imagine that coming home and telling Maggie that I had signed a particular contract or filled an unusually large order or mediated a silly dispute between two secretaries would improve my marriage. But we both feel the difference.

Many of the things that Shawn shares with Maggie about his day at work could be characterized as small talk; topics range from the brand of coffee they use in the vending machines to the latest office romance. But this so-called small talk has had a beneficial impact on their marriage because Maggie feels more connected to Shawn.

Big Talk Is Necessary

We presume that the opposite of small talk is big talk. For us, big talk involves such matters as worries, fears, anxieties, aspirations, hopes, dreams, hurts, anger, frustrations, and issues about which you have conflict. As we noted, small talk is necessary but, in some cases, can be a way to avoid the bigger issues. We know two people, a couple married for nine years, who are almost totally alienated from each other even though they continue to live together. The only conversations they have involve small talk—"It's rainy today"; "Did you pay the rent?"; "We need milk." In their case, small talk diminishes rather than enhances intimacy. They use the small talk to avoid talking about the problems that have corroded their marriage.

When small talk is combined with big talk, however, you are on your way to an exciting union. But despite the benefits, many couples avoid discussions about the big issues. It may require a good deal of time to resolve one of these issues, and you are already trying to cram twenty-eight hours of living into every twenty-four-hour day. They may generate conflict and who wants to fight when life is already so hectic? Or who wants to acknowledge feelings of inadequacy, fear, or anxiety—even to a mate?

Recall that Shawn said he didn't want to burden Maggie with his work problems. Further discussion revealed that he also didn't want Maggie to know about some of the mistakes he had made at work; he feared she might criticize him, and he had already endured enough criticism from his boss.

So there are risks in talking about the bigger things—the risk that your spouse will be dismayed by your weakness, or that you will get into an argument, or that you will spend so much time talking about an issue that you neglect other important matters. Nevertheless, the risks must be accepted. And once they are, you will probably experience a feeling of liberation. A man married nineteen years put it this way:

> For a long time, I didn't talk to my wife about my frustrations and fears of inadequacy at work. I knew she had an image of me as someone who was really competent, and I liked her to think about me that way. But I had to talk to someone, so I finally opened up to her. What a relief! She encouraged me and supported me. It not only helped me get through a tough time at work, but also made our relationship better than ever.

Their relationship became "better than ever" because his wife now knew more about him than she had before— a man with needs and frailties as well as appealing strengths. And he knew more about his wife—a woman with the capacity to stand by him and be a source of strength for him and whose love for him was not contingent upon him being flawless.

That's the point of talking about the bigger matters—

you really get to know each other. And keep in mind that the bigger matters are not confined to problems. Sharing your dreams and aspirations, talking about things that move you deeply, and exploring ideas are some of the matters that open you up to each other so that your lives become increasingly intertwined in intimate union.

Dean discovered, to his delight, that after he and Terry began their scheduled, intimate talks, he often felt afterward as if he had gotten a "jolt of joy":

> You don't even have to talk about yourselves. Sometimes Terry and I will discuss something that's going on, like a newspaper story about gang violence. And we each talk about how the whole thing makes us feel and what we think could be done about it. Or sometimes we talk about our church, and how we each feel about one of the services. And afterward, I feel really good about our marriage. Closer to Terry. Like we just did something great together.

There are a number of reasons why Dean feels as he does. And why everyone gets such a boost from discussing the bigger matters:

- You are making yourself vulnerable, thereby affirming your trust in your partner;
- You are giving a part of yourself to your partner that you withhold from most others, thereby affirming your desire for intimacy;
- You are giving time to your relationship, thereby affirming your commitment to your partner.

How Can You Protect Your Talk Against Busyness?

Even if you schedule times to talk together, you need to be careful to protect your times of conversation, for busyness can subvert them in a number of ways. You might find yourself, for instance, only halfheartedly involved because of the pressing urgency of some other demands. You might find it difficult to concentrate on what your partner is saying because intrusive thoughts keep popping into your mind. You might be too weary to be fully engaged in the conversation.

We suggest a number of things you can do to protect against the subversive effects of busyness:

1. *Remind yourself that this conversation is a crucial part of following through with your primary commitment (chapter 2).* This will help you resist distracting thoughts and the sense that you really should be doing something else.

Don't minimize the importance of this suggestion. It involves what psychologists call self-talk, a useful technique for helping yourself deal with all kinds of situations. Terry uses this self-talk to get her in the right frame of mind for intimate talk:

> Once in a while I get to feeling more pressured than usual, and I would just as soon be doing something other than sitting down and talking with Dean. So I just tell myself that this is as important as anything else I have to do, that it is part of my commitment to this marriage, and that it is going to make our marriage better and better.

After telling herself such things, Terry reports, she is usually able to put aside the other pressures in her life and to feel enthused about the conversation.

2. *Schedule your conversations for a time when you won't be at a low ebb physically and/or emotionally.* Don't make the mistake of thinking that talking can be done at just any time. If you want to get the maximum

intimacy benefit from your conversations, have them at a time when you can be fully and energetically engaged with each other. Small talk may work when you are tired, but enriching conversations require energized talkers.

One couple responded to this suggestion by asserting that they only saw each other when one or the other of them was weary:

> I feel great in the mornings, but he's a drag until he's been up for an hour and had his coffee. And then it's time to go to work. He feels great in the evenings, but I'm usually wrung out. And the dinner hour is the time we give to our children. So when do we talk about these big issues you say we need to discuss? When I'm beat or when he's beat?

Our response to such a question is this. First, remember your primary commitment. Second, you have just as much time as everyone else in the world—twenty-four hours every day. Third, make sure you are managing your time well; many couples make additional time for themselves by following the suggestions made in chapter 4. Fourth, you may be right. Perhaps even after using all the good time-management techniques, you have nothing left for each other. Then it's time to practice your primary commitment and raise the question of what you are going to cut out of your life so that you make time for each other.

Faced with such a challenge, the couple thought about it and agreed to come up with some way to find time for intimate talk. They found it when the husband agreed to get up an hour earlier in the morning, pump his mind up with some coffee, and spend time with his wife before going to work.

3. *Don't allow verbal skirting to consume your time.* Verbal skirting is talking around a particular issue without ever getting to the real point. Busy people can't allow ver-

bal skirting to consume valuable time that could be used for intimate talk. An example of verbal skirting is the following conversation, in which the husband really wanted to bring up the issue of his desire for more frequent sex:

He: Is there anything wrong?

She: What makes you think that?

He: I don't know. You seem to be really busy lately.

She: Not any more than usual.

He: It just seems like you are.

She: Why do you say that?

He: I don't know. There's not a lot of time for things.

She: There never is enough time.

He: Yeah.

And so on. By the time he gets to the point, if he ever does, they will have consumed valuable time. She may even get irritated with him for having skirted around the issue and leaving no time to actually discuss it.

Incidentally, don't confuse verbal skirting with what we call connecting through verbal ambling. At one time, Shawn believed that Maggie was engaging in verbal skirting when she talked at length about something. "I kept wanting her to get to the point," he said. He didn't realize that the point was that Maggie enjoyed connecting with him by sharing the full details with him. There was no point to be made, except the point of building intimacy through verbal ambling.

4. *Look at your partner.* People in love tend to look into each other's eyes. Couples in trouble frequently avoid looking at each other. Looking at each other, then, is a way to affirm love. It is also a way to pick up the nonverbal aspects of the conversation, to note all those facial movements and expressions that convey so much information and enable you to understand better what your spouse is saying. In short, looking at your partner makes the most of your intimate talk time.

Some people get into a habit of not looking at each other. It doesn't mean they no longer love each other. Rather, the habit may reflect that they are taking their relationship for granted. If you have fallen into this habit, looking at your partner will put new vigor into your conversations and into your relationship.

In other cases, the failure to look at each other may be rooted in busyness; so many things are going through your mind that they tear your eyes away from your partner. If you really look at your partner, it will help you to put distracting thoughts aside and enhance the quality of your talk. It's hard to look directly at someone and think about a thousand other things.

Swirling thoughts in his busy mind were one reason Shawn had trouble listening to Maggie, even when they were talking about something serious or were involved in an argument. One day in the midst of a disagreement, Maggie stopped and said to him: "I need you to look at me." She was right. She sensed that at least some of what she said was not getting through to him. She also had difficulty gauging his reaction to what she was saying because his eyes were averted.

What neither realized at the time was that her need was also his need. Only when he looked at her did Shawn begin to understand the depth of her distress about the issue. And only when he looked at her did he feel fully involved in and equally responsible for resolving the issue.

5. *Don't let your conversations be dominated by prob-*

lems or negative topics. At times, of course, you will have to deal with marital problems, with problems in the family or at work, and with various kinds of negative topics. But don't let such things dominate your intimate talk. To do so is to punish yourselves for talking together. And you're too busy to continue something that is basically a punitive experience.

Some couples deal with this by scheduling a particular time that is given only to a discussion of problems or any troublesome things in their lives. At other times, they focus on matters that are interesting, entertaining, uplifting, or enjoyable.

6. *Practice a daily word of affirmation.* This is the flip side of the last suggestion. As Paul put it: "Let no evil talk come out of your mouths, but only what is useful for building up, as there is need, so that your words may give grace to those who hear" (Ephesians 4:29). Every marriage needs a daily dose of grace. You maximize the value of your talk when you include at some time a word of grace to your spouse, an affirmation in the form of something you appreciate, admire, or value in your spouse. Build each other up in talk. It's a great way to build intimacy and to fill your days together with grace.

Take Time To . . .

1. Find yourselves a special "couple's place" in your home. It doesn't have to be anything elaborate—the living room sofa, a stack of pillows propped on your bed, a porch swing or the chaise lounge on your patio, or the kitchen table will do. The important thing is to have a place—free as possible from the distraction of television, telephone,

and even kids—that you associate with intimate talk. And then, of course, to use it.

2. Develop the art of small talk. As you go about the activities of the day, make note of fun and trivial things to share with your spouse at dinner or when you talk that evening. This is a great way to enjoy each other.

3. Schedule a specific time each week to discuss problems. This isn't always possible because some problems require an immediate response. But it's helpful to postpone recurring issues or nonemergency concerns—like how to keep our expenditures from consistently exceeding our earnings, or are we going to spend the holidays at your parents or mine, or should we start a family this year or next—until this scheduled time. It will keep you from obsessing about the problem all week and reassure you that the issue will soon be handled.

9

Little Things Mean a Lot

"Better is a little with righteousness than large income with injustice."

Proverbs 16:8

"And whoever gives even a cup of cold water to one of these little ones in the name of a disciple—truly I tell you, none of these will lose their reward." *Matthew 10:42*

> *"The most romantic thing my husband ever did? We've had a lot of romance in our marriage. The thing that comes to mind—and you may think this sounds silly—is the time he sent me an unexpected love letter."*
> *Janet—wife, mother of four, homemaker*
>
> *"We try to make some kind of love contact with each other every day. On days when I know that we are going to have very little time together, I call Sheila at work just to ask how her day is going and to tell her I love her."*
> *Jack—husband, accountant, father*

How much time and how much money does it take to build intimacy in your marriage? Some people despair because they believe the answer is "a lot," or at least "more than I've got." Not so. The Bible urges us to remember the value of little things. To paraphrase Proverbs, it's better to have little wealth and good relationships than to amass a lot of money and relate unjustly to others. And Jesus reminded us at various times about the value of little things—the importance of giving a cup of cold water and the value of the widow's small offering (Mark 12:42).

Janet underscored the value of little things for us when she said that a cherished romantic moment for her was receiving an unexpected love letter from her husband, Dave. What did that letter cost? About ten minutes in time and the price of a postage stamp. So think about some of the little ways in which you can build intimacy. Like the mustard seed, which is "the smallest of all the seeds, but when it has grown it is the greatest of shrubs and becomes a tree. . . ." (Matthew 13:32), little acts of intimacy can grow into strong bonds of love.

Court Your Spouse

The next time you have an opportunity to "people watch," take a few minutes to observe the behavior of couples. Can you separate the married from the dating couples? How can you tell? The dating couples, you say, seem much more attentive and courteous to each other. And you may be right. Unfortunately, for many couples, the niceties of dating and courtship vanish at the altar. It's as if "I do" also means "I no longer have to."

We observed a couple, whom we knew quite well, arriving at a church function. The husband got out of the car, walked nearly half a block, then looked around and asked with a touch of annoyance in his voice, "Where's DeeDee?" He hadn't noticed that she was still at the car, picking up items she had dropped from her purse. In all fairness, this couple seems to have a good marriage; the loss of some of the courtesies of courtship doesn't mean that their marriage is doomed. So DeeDee shrugged off her husband's behavior. But she would have felt so much better if he had waited for her, helped her, walked hand in hand with her—because no one ever gets weary of loving consideration.

We're not suggesting that you become as consumed

with each other as you were during courtship, only that
you continue—or bring back—some of the thoughtful and
romantic ways you each behaved then. To court your
spouse, try such things as:

- Make physical contact daily—kiss, hug, cuddle,
  hold hands.
- Give ongoing love messages—express love both
  verbally and nonverbally—touch, eye contact,
  facial expressions.
- Surprise your spouse with small gifts—a perfect
  apple, a rose, a compact disc, a favorite maga-
  zine, or whatever will bring a smile of delight.
- Do something unexpected—prepare a meal you
  normally would not fix; relieve your spouse of
  a chore he or she hates to do; plan a special
  date or vacation.
- Give your spouse a voucher, good for a dinner
  out or an hour or two of free time.
- Re-create a romantic experience from when
  you were dating.

Note that some of the above suggestions take time, but
others require very little or no additional time. It takes no
extra time, for example, to affirm your love by smiling at
your spouse. A loving smile is one of those little things
that multiply in value. When we asked Jack to reflect upon
some particularly meaningful experiences he has had with
Sheila in their twenty-two year-marriage, he reflected a
moment then said:

> The thing I treasure most is the way Sheila always
> has a smile for me at just the right moment. Her
> smile defuses my anger and reminds me not to take
> myself so seriously. I remember during the early
> years, I would often come home from work really
> frazzled. And she would smile at me, and that

smile said to me: "It's okay. I love you. I support you. I will stand by you." And her smile still works magic for me.

A smile, a hug, a kind word, a simple courtesy—little things that work magic in relationships. They are genuine bargains. They cost little to nothing and are guaranteed relationship enhancers.

Laugh and Play Together

People with fulfilling marriages laugh and play together. Laughter and play are signs of intimacy and, at the same time, they build intimacy. When you laugh together, when you are playful together, you work as a team to reduce life's tensions and renew your spirits. For busy people, who can easily fall into a habit of being serious about everything as they rush about the business of life, laughter and playfulness are like powerful vitamins that build both your personal and your marital health. And it takes no more time to laugh about something than it does to growl about it.

There are, however, helpful and hurtful ways of laughing and playing in a relationship. It's important to know the difference.

It's Not Always Fun to Laugh

Some kinds of laughter and playfulness are counterproductive. The following rules may seem unnecessary to you—we hope they do—but we know couples who consistently break them:

1. *Don't laugh at your partner; laugh with your partner.* Laughing at a spouse's mistake or shortcoming adds hurt to the embarrassment that he or she probably already feels. Used as criticism or derision, laughter can cut more deeply than words.

2. *Don't use laughter to trivialize your partner's emo-*

tions or feelings about something. We heard a husband laugh as he talked about his wife's sensitivity to remarks that one of his friends made about her. "She takes it too seriously," he said. "It isn't that important." But it clearly was important to her, and when he tried to laugh it off he merely added to her distress.

3. *Don't use laughter to try to neutralize an offense.* Jack acknowledges that earlier in his marriage, he did this with Sheila:

> When I was tired, I didn't have much patience. I would say something hurtful to Sheila when she annoyed me. Instead of admitting that I was wrong, I tried to take the sting out of my words by laughing and saying that I was only kidding. Sometimes it worked. More often it didn't, and then we'd either stop talking to each other for awhile or end up in an argument.

4. *Don't confuse teasing with humor and playfulness.* Stan, who has been married for two years, wants to create a home filled with laughter and fun. But it hasn't been an easy task for him, mainly because of his father's example. About the only laughter he heard at home while he was growing up was at someone's expense and most of the playfulness came in the form of teasing. Some of Stan's earliest memories are of his father teasing him by dangling a toy just out of his reach. And as he grew up, Stan remembers that his father teased him about everything from his appearance to his clumsiness around girls.

Stan didn't realize how much he had been shaped by his father's approach to humor until his wife confronted him one day with the fact that he often did to her what his father had done to him:

> She reminded me that I always teased her about getting fat whenever she ate a hamburger and

fries and constantly poked fun at her because she wasn't very mechanical. Things like that. I really thought we were just having fun together until she told me how much some of these remarks hurt her. I still occasionally fall into the old practice of teasing, but I'm really working on ridding myself of this destructive habit.

These four rules deal with the kinds of things that are *not* humor and playfulness. Now let's look at what we mean by humor and playfulness and how to use them.

Learn to Have Fun While Building Intimacy

In essence, humor and playfulness in marriage are shared experiences of fun that make you feel closer together and good about each other. We include everything from sharing a cartoon or joke that struck you as funny to playful wrestling with each other to doing something that might be called "mischievous." By mischievous, we mean doing something that your stern uncle and aunt would frown upon as frivolous—like having a pillow fight, or sneaking a midnight snack, or taking a day off when you should be working.

Of course, to paraphrase an old saying, one spouse's humor can be the other spouse's annoyance. You may enjoy a pillow fight, but it might only be annoying to your spouse. That's the kind of thing you each learn by trial and error. Respect your spouse's sense of humor, of course; then try to add a daily dose of humor to your life. Among other things, you could:

- Share with each other anything funny that happens during the day.
- Recall fun times in the past. This gives you the chance to enjoy them a second time.
- When you go out somewhere, pretend you're on a

date with the task of making each other laugh and having a good time.

- Do something silly or frivolous—do an imitation of a difficult person you know, reenact for your spouse an embarrassing moment you had, take the phone off the hook so you can have some privacy, go for a walk in the rain, share a quart (actually, a half gallon would be more frivolous) of your favorite ice cream.

Use Humor and Playfulness to Connect

We have talked about the importance of connecting with each other regularly. Humor and playfulness are one way to do that. To be sure, there is a good deal of seriousness to life in general and to marriage in particular. You don't want to trivialize serious matters. At the same time, there is usually a humorous side to many weighty situations. And life has to be more than the somber, burdensome stuff. All seriousness and no play makes marriage a very dull affair.

When you connect with each other in fun, you build a unique and important kind of intimacy. After all, isn't it the people you have fun with, the people you laugh with, that you want to be around? They touch your life with lightness and cheer. And the point is, you can and should do the same for your spouse.

Use Humor and Playfulness to Keep Your Bearings

Humor and playfulness are also important in coping with difficult situations and keeping them in perspective. They give you a buoyancy that keeps you from being pulled under by the difficulties that come to all of us. Janet gave us an example:

> Dave's stepmother, Roberta, is a real pill, and we both know it. We've had some arguments about

the situation, though, because Dave wants to get along with her; he's afraid he will hurt his father's feelings if he doesn't. We've had a lot of serious talks about the situation and believe that it's one that we can't change. We just have to learn to live with it.

Several months ago, Roberta was again the topic of our discussion. Dave was irritated because Roberta was so sarcastic. She gets down on everything, especially church. She doesn't like the pastor, hates the music, and complains about the format of the worship service. Instead of chiming in the way I usually do, I said, "Why don't we each take a Bible the next time we go to her house, and stand at the door and serenade her with the doxology?" It was a silly thing to say, but it just popped into my head. For some reason, Dave just cracked up at the prospect of our doing this. Like two naughty kids, we came up with several more mischievous ways we could respond to Roberta's tirades and laughed about every one of them. Instead of feeling glum and hopeless afterward, like we usually do when Roberta's the topic of conversation, we felt relaxed and in good spirits.

This incident illustrates how to use humor and playfulness to deal with some of the vexing matters in life without trivializing their importance. Roberta's still a problem, and Janet and Dave are still concerned about keeping peace in the family. But as long as they can laugh about the situation, the problem won't overwhelm them.

Become Your Spouse's Cheerleader

Most of you learned as you were growing up how to be critics. Parents and teachers alike were more likely to point out your wrong turns than to applaud your right ones. Researchers observing parents interacting with their children have found that parents give far more words of direction and reproof than of praise to their children. And probably many of you had teachers who noted every mistake but rarely or never praised creative or even error-free work.

The upshot is that many people come to marriage well equipped to be a critic but having an underdeveloped sense of how to be a cheerleader. They tend to be vocal about the displeasing things that their spouses say and do, but are likely to watch in silence when their spouses are performing well.

We urge you to reverse this pattern, so that your spouse hears far more positive and approving things from you than negative and critical ones. An excellent way to cement your union for life is to become each other's cheerleader. Just recall the times in your life when someone praised or encouraged or thanked you. Think about how you felt. No one ever gets weary of, or ever loses the need to hear, such affirmation. Just as we want to be around people who make us laugh, we want to be with those who value and appreciate us.

There's a delightful scene in the play and movie *Fiddler on the Roof,* where Tevye asks his wife if she loves him. She replies by reminding him of how many years she has taken care of him and their family. But he persists with the question, for he needs to hear the words, "I love you."

We're all much the same. We need to hear words of love and affirmation from our spouses. So become your spouse's cheerleader. Among other things:

1. *Applaud your spouse's achievements.* By achievements, we mean everything from success at work to mastering a new skill to handling a difficult situation well. A female friend of ours returned to school to complete her college education after her children were grown. Her feelings of joy at what she was achieving were frayed by her

husband's reaction: "I try to tell him some of the things I'm learning in my psychology class, and he just puts them down as dumb." Even if he disagreed with some of the content of what she was learning, he could have muted his criticisms and praised her enthusiasm and her intellectual development. It would have taken no more time than his cynical dismissal, and it would have added a halo of joy to his wife and to their marriage.

2. *Compliment your spouse from time to time on things you admire about him or her.* And don't take it for granted that your words are superfluous. A wife told us:

> We had been married eight years when my hus-
> band told me how nice I looked one morning as I
> was leaving for work. I nearly fainted because he
> never seemed to notice what I wore or how I
> looked. I thanked him, but also told him how
> amazed I was by his compliment. He said I always
> seemed so confident about my appearance that he
> felt it wasn't necessary to tell me how good I
> always looked. But I told him that it was really
> important to me to hear the words from him.

It's a relatively simple matter to say such things as: "You did a good job"; "I love the way you make people feel so welcome when they come to our home"; "I really look forward to coming home to your meals"; "I like the way you lay your head on my shoulder when you're tired"; "You are so loving with the kids, even when you discipline them." So in addition to a laugh a day, give your spouse a compliment every day.

3. *Follow the rules of courtesy with your spouse.* Acts of courtesy and thoughtfulness that you accord to others should also be given to your spouse. These include saying "please" and "thank you," holding a door open, offering to get something your spouse needs or would like (such as a coat or a napkin), pouring your spouse an extra cup of

coffee rather than waiting for him or her to get it. Such small acts send an important message: "I care about you and am sensitive to your needs." Little things really do mean a lot.

Keep at It When You're Apart

There's an opportunity for strengthening your marriage that doesn't even occur to many couples—the times when you are separated. Of course, most of your intimacy building will occur when you are together. But there are a number of ways to sustain and even build intimacy while you are separated, whether the separation is during the daily work hours or for a more extended period of time.

Make Daily Separation Work for You

Most couples go their separate ways during the day. But you can even use this time apart to enhance your relationship. Here are a number of possibilities for making the most of your time apart:

1. *Make your departure and return an intimate moment.* Which of the following comes closest to your practice?

- The only way she knows when he has gone and returned is hearing the door slam.
- She leaves first, shouting a "see ya" as she runs out the door. He returns last, shouting "I'm home" as he sits down and reads the mail.
- Every parting and return is marked by a hug and kiss.

Need we say which is the preferred pattern?

2. *Keep visible reminders near you.* Keep pictures of your spouse and family on your desk. And look at the pictures. A man told us: "I call the corner of my desk my

smile corner. Every time I look at my family, it brings a smile to my face."

You should also surround yourself with objects that remind you of your spouse. Of course, there's your wedding ring—a symbol of your love and commitment to each other. But there are also other possibilities—a pinecone from a park where you walk together, a memento from your most recent vacation, a framed copy of a poem your spouse wrote for you on your last anniversary. Like the medieval knights who carried with them a piece of material from the clothing of their beloved, such an object can remind you of your commitment to each other.

3. *Use the telephone.* Jack has the right idea when he makes a "love contact" by calling Sheila from work just to tell her he loves her. Another couple told us that they frequently connect during the day via their mobile phones. Both of their jobs require them to drive a great deal so they use these opportunities to check in and see "how things are going." And, of course, the answering machine offers creative possibilities for leaving your spouse a loving message.

4. *Talk about your spouse and family with coworkers when it's appropriate to do so.* Obviously, we aren't advocating that you interrupt your next business meeting with an account of your husband's latest culinary triumphs. But we overheard a nice example one day when a young woman said to her boss, "You really look sharp today." He thanked her. He could have let it go at that. But he added with a smile: "Whenever I look nice, give my wife the credit. She's the one with taste in our family."

It seems a small thing. But more than one affair has begun with a man or woman making admiring and complimentary remarks to a colleague. And more than one marriage has been second rate because the partners never think of each other except when they're together—and not always then.

5. *Do something unexpected.* A wife saw her husband's car at their health club as she was driving to a business appointment. She wrote him a love note and put it in the car. A husband who is a salesman frequently passes by the office building where his wife works. Every so often he stops in and brings her a cappucino or just walks up to her, kisses her, and walks away without a word. A wife occasionally uses part of her lunch hour to think about something she appreciates about her husband; she writes her thoughts down and leaves them on his pillow.

Use Longer Separations to Your Advantage

For many couples, daily separation is the least of their worries. Work or family responsibilities require that they be separated for extended periods of time. How can you maintain your intimate connection if you have to be away from your spouse for a lengthy period of time? First of all, make parting and returning memorable moments. When our friend Raoul recently had to leave on a two-week business trip, he cooked a surprise dinner, complete with roses and candles, for his wife the night before his departure. His wife said this about her memories of the dinner:

> Thinking about that dinner kept Raoul with me the whole time he was gone. Every time I smelled the roses or even thought about the mess he left in the kitchen, my heart just sang with love for him. So I decided to make his homecoming special, too. His plane landed very late so I decided to give him the "royal treatment" the next morning—breakfast in bed with blueberry pancakes, his absolute favorite, and freshly squeezed orange juice. He was thrilled.

Second, maintain your connections when you're away. Don't forget the pictures. A photo of your spouse and children can brighten even the dreariest hotel room. Use the telephone to span the distance between you. Make sure your calls are not merely a report of what's going on, but also an affirmation of each other. Instead of a terse "I miss you," try something like "I really miss holding you close to me" or "I really miss seeing your smile when I come in at the end of the day." And don't overlook the value of the mail. A wife who receives a daily postcard from her husband whenever he is gone for more than two days says, "I love his notes and look forward to them, even if some of them arrive after he is already back home."

Finally, leave a surprise for your spouse to discover. If you are the one left behind, put a surprise in your partner's luggage. If you are the one traveling, leave something behind. Sophia's family are all in Europe. She met her husband, Charley, while he was working for an international corporation that has its headquarters in her hometown. They now live in the United States, but Sophia spends a couple of months each year in Europe with her family. The trips are important to her, but she is also determined not to let them jeopardize her marriage. Among other things, just before she leaves she writes a number of love notes and puts them into Charley's pockets and other places where he is likely—sooner or later—to discover them. Each time he finds one of the notes, Charley feels the warmth of his wife's love. Neither of them prefers the separations, but they make the most of them. They have learned to stay close even when they are far apart.

Take Time To . . .

1. Plan to do the unexpected in your marriage. "Whoa!" you say. "Isn't that a contradiction in terms? If you plan it,

how can it be unexpected?" To a large extent, of course, you are correct. But as busy as you are, if you don't plan surprises they just won't happen. So we recommend that you cultivate a mind-set that welcomes the occasional zany, novel, unique experience. Be on the lookout for opportunities to do something different, something that is out of the ordinary for you.

2. Start the tradition of bringing home a memento from your vacations or special times together to put on your office desk. The simpler the better—a polished stone, a sea shell, a theater program, a restaurant menu, a favorite photograph. When you look at this memento, remember your spouse and the special times you share.

3. Use your wedding ring as a mental reminder of your spouse and of your mutual commitment. For example, whenever you wash and dry your hands, see the ring's reflection in the mirror, or twist it on your finger, remember your spouse and thank God for bringing you together.

4. Think of ways to keep close when you are away from each other for an extended period. For example, spend time together (even if it's just on the ride to the airport) before you part. Always send the traveling spouse off with a warm passionate kiss (a quick peck on the cheek just isn't enough). Use the telephone to keep in touch while you are away; a morning and/or an evening call will let your spouse know that he or she is in your thoughts. And mark your reunion in a special way—a small gift from your travels, a family welcoming party to meet the plane, a quiet evening together. Keep it low key; reentry is often exhausting.

10

And Big Things Mean a Lot, Too

"For you tithe mint, dill, and cummin, and have neglected the weightier matters of the law: justice and mercy and faith. It is these you ought to have practiced without neglecting the others."

Matthew 23:23

> *"I always thought that sex should be spontaneous—like we'd be doing something at home, suddenly look at each other, feel overwhelmed by desire, and jump into bed. And once there we would spend an hour in passion and romance. Well, if we waited for that to happen, we'd be living celibate lives."*
>
> Cindy—wife, paralegal, mother
>
> *"We've had a lot of problems, but we've always helped each other through the power of God's words. We've come through a lot of storms because we study the Bible together and then try to live out its teachings in our daily lives. Our marriage is living proof that God is sufficient!"*
>
> Vic—husband, contractor, father

He offended her by once again losing his temper and berating her. He tried to ease the tension by mumbling "I'm sorry" and excusing his behavior with a joke. She didn't laugh. The next time he lashed out at her, he again mumbled a quick apology. The following day he sent her flowers.

She put them aside and didn't look at them. The verbal abuse had been going on too long. Jokes and flowers could not repair the damage.

The point is, little things mean a lot, but only when the big things have also been taken care of. Jesus made this point when he condemned the scribes and Pharisees because, although they tithed, they "neglected the weightier matters of the law: justice and mercy and faith. It is these you ought to have practiced without neglecting the others" (Matthew 23:23).

We've already considered some of the big things, like commitment, conflict, and communication. Let's look at three others that are particularly challenging for busy couples but also fundamental to the quality of their marriage: sex, special events, and spiritual development.

Can You Be Both Busy and Sexy?

The great majority of busy couples say that their sex lives are negatively affected by their schedules. Many are so worn out by evening that they have no energy or even interest left for sex. As a young mother said in one of our discussion groups, "I often feel at the end of the day like sex is just one *more* thing I have to do." "Yes," said her husband, "and I feel like it's just one more thing I *have* to do."

If it's any consolation, often couples report having more and better sex after years of marriage than when they were first married. But "more and better" doesn't necessarily mean "as much as I'd like" or "as much as I need." Keep in mind that the busier you are, the less likely you are to *feel* sexual. That doesn't mean you don't *need* sex as much. As one busy husband put it:

> I sometimes get so consumed by work, family,
> church, and my professional organizations that I
> hardly even think about sex. The longer I go
> without it, however, the crankier I become. I get

short tempered with the kids and with my wife. And she starts feeling edgy, too. After we have sex, we both feel like new people and much better able to cope with life.

As he illustrates, the problem of sex for busy people is not just having enough time. It's also a problem of staying alert to your sexual needs and of keeping passion alive. The following suggestions, therefore, are intended not only to help you find time but also to increase the awareness of your need and to stimulate your desire for sexual fulfillment.

Have Sensual Conversations

Sensual conversations are not necessarily about sex. Like many busy mothers and wives, Cindy finds herself going several days without even thinking about sex. Her husband, Jeff, generally takes the initiative in reigniting the sexual spark in their marriage:

I can tell when Jeff really wants sex. He gets a kind of hungry look in his eyes. And his touch becomes a bit more demanding. We touch a lot anyway, but it's different when he wants to make love. Sometimes I'm just not ready. I need to shift gears emotionally and mentally. So I ask him for a little time together. He knows that means we need some time for other kinds of intimacy. Often he'll make us a pot of tea. As we sit and drink the tea together, we talk about all sorts of things. Recently, we discussed next summer's vacation. As we talked and I watched him, I felt more and more sexy. He was in the middle of a sentence when I interrupted him and said, "Let's go to bed."

If you have good communication, if you really connect with each other verbally, your conversations are sensual because they are an important foundation for sexual desire. At times, however, you may also want to have explicit sexual discussions. For example, one of the items on the survey of intimacy needs in chapter 3 was your sexual relationship. This is a good beginning for further exploration of this issue. Talk together about your sexual needs, sexual desires, and the kinds of things that stir up sexual passion. Sometimes, talking is all you need to stoke up your sexual desire for one another.

Practice Sensual Behavior

Like sensual conversations, sensual behavior is anything that makes you feel closer together whether or not it is directly related to sex. A husband told us that his wife makes love to him all the time, expressing gratitude for having him in her life, caring for him and their family in hundreds of ways, and routinely showering him with affection. This is sensual behavior.

Conversely, any behavior that detracts from intimacy will depress your sexual relationship. A wife gave us an example of such nonsensual behavior:

> We've had a good sexual relationship most of our married life. The only time it hasn't been good was when the kids were young. Especially the year after our third child was born. I was exhausted. I didn't feel that my husband was pulling his share of the load. I really resented this, and my resentment killed my sexual desire. When we worked through the problem and he became more involved in helping with the kids, our sex life really improved.

For most people, sex is a big issue. But in sex, as in other matters, little things mean a lot. So don't overlook all the little things that keep rekindling sexual desire. A few things that couples find helpful are:

- Kiss with feeling rather than merely giving your spouse a peck on the cheek—it only takes a few seconds longer.
- Write your spouse a passionate love note.
- Shower together.
- Touch and caress each other a lot.
- Develop your own code language for sex—such as "How about some really special dessert tonight?"

Be Creative

Perhaps the biggest problem for you is not desire but time. If this is the case, it's time to be creative. Some couples keep waiting for a break in their full schedule when the sex will simply happen. But like intimacy, generally, you can't wait for it to happen. You have to take charge of your life. Put your imagination to work and find the necessary time to have a more fulfilling sex life. Among other things, busy couples should consider two things:

(1) Schedule your sexual encounters. To some people, "scheduled sex" already sounds like half the fun is gone. But if it's a choice between scheduled sex and no sex, which would you prefer? Scheduling sex doesn't mean you can never be spontaneous. A busy professional woman once did something she still blushes about: "I had some time to spare and I knew my husband had a flexible schedule that day. I went to a hotel near his office, rented a room, then called and invited him to join me for the afternoon. And he did." Another couple tells how they occasionally, and spontaneously, call off an evening engagement, bring in some dinner, take a bubble bath together, and leisurely make love.

Spontaneous acts like these add a lot of spice to a marriage, but they're completely impossible for some couples and no one can do them regularly. So you're back to scheduling—the same as you do for everything else that is important to you. Some couples make long-range plans; they schedule regular times during the week when they typically have sexual relations. But you can make short-range plans as well, scheduling time for lovemaking in the minutes or hours ahead. You might say to your spouse, for instance, "How about going to bed early tonight and making love?" which is far better than hoping your spouse will realize that you need sex and will initiate it.

But can you really schedule sexual relations? What if the scheduled time arrives and you're too weary or not in the mood? First, if you know it's scheduled you can usually get yourself into the mood by turning off other thoughts and concerns, reserving some energy, and concentrating on making love. Second, you need not hold rigidly to any schedule. Occasionally, you might decide to cuddle and talk instead, with the promise of an exciting encounter the next time.

(2) Make sexual fulfillment a challenging adventure. Is sex something that should be done in the dark? Only in a particular place? Only when you have at least an hour? No, no, and no. Get rid of all the stereotypes about sexual behavior. Couples with a fulfilling sexual life find all sorts of ways to find time for making love. We counseled a couple with a typical problem—too little sex. In this case, it was the wife who was complaining. The husband said he was just too weary from work to feel sexual at bedtime. The couple was recently married and had no children. We asked why they didn't consider making love in the morning. A light went on in their eyes. It was something they had not even considered. Some months later we saw the wife and asked her how married life was now. "Great!"

Other couples are similarly creative. Their sexual encounters range from quick (ten minutes or less) encounters anywhere in the house any time of the day to longer times with the telephone turned off and the kids at their grandparents. Quick sex may not be as satisfying as more leisurely lovemaking, but, like scheduled sex, it is better than no sex at all.

There are other ways to be creative. The point is, rather than waiting and hoping for something to happen that will give you time for making love, you must sit down together and brainstorm ways to get sexual fulfillment. You will probably discover that there are more options than you thought.

Plan Some Special Events

Yes, these are going to require some time. But keep three things in mind: You won't do them that often; they'll be very rewarding; and even the planning is fun. In fact, they're more than rewarding. They are a way to protect your marriage against one of its enemies—boring routine. Even sex becomes a dull routine for some people when they always make love in the same way, the same place, and the same time. And among people who divorce after many years of marriage, a substantial number give boredom as one of the reasons for the breakup.

Ironically, the busier you are, the more susceptible you may be to boredom in your marriage. For if your marriage is routine while your life generally is exciting even though hectic, the contrast will work to the detriment of the marriage. Special events are one way to ensure against marital apathy.

What are special events? Basically, whatever is special to you. It may be a special vacation for which you have to plan and save. A couple told us about their one and only trip to Europe:

> We had to borrow money to go. It took us a number of years to pay it off. But we have no regrets. We know a lot of other people who would love to go, but still haven't made it. We've been there, and it was great.

Special events need not be that elaborate or costly. They can include such things as:

- A weekend away for just the two of you
- A weekday picnic and hike
- A special date at a favorite restaurant to cele-brate something significant—or insignificant, for that matter
- An occasional surprise date with each partner alternating responsibility for planning what to do and where to go

Finally, we suggest that you consider a do-it-yourself enrichment weekend. A note of caution—this should *not* be a let's-solve-our-problems weekend. At any point in your marriage, you are likely to have an issue or problem that you would like to resolve. But for this kind of week-end, suspend any thoughts about or attempts to settle such matters. Focus, instead, on having fun together, learning more about each other, and sharing intimate experiences.

For instance, a couple came to us frustrated by their schedules. "We really would like to attend a marriage enrichment program," the wife said. "But whenever they're scheduled, we can't make it. And when we can make it, there isn't one available." We suggested that they try a marriage enrichment weekend on their own. We gave them some materials, showed them how to use them, and they took off on their marital adventure. The wife summed up the experience in three words: "It was wonderful."

As it turned out, they only used one of the materials we gave them. It was a personality test that can be self-scored. They each took it, then each answered it for the other. They talked about the similarities and differences in their self-perceptions and spouse-perceptions. That is, she didn't see herself quite the way that he saw her, and vice versa. They talked about how the results influenced their rela-tionship, and about how they could use their new under-standing to enrich their marriage. They got so involved in the personality test and the discussion it provoked that they didn't have time to use the rest of the materials we provided. They are saving them for the next time, and they both agree "there will be a next time!"

There are various ways you can construct such a weekend for yourself. Many churches provide suggested readings and activities for marriage enrichment. Another way is to get a book on marriage, such as our *For Better and Better*, and work through a number of the chapters. Read them, discuss the content and how it applies to your relationship, and do the suggested activities. Or you might prefer to work around a theme. Your theme could be love, or sex, or aspirations and hopes, or having fun together, or whatever. Explore the theme by each of you writing down and then discussing the following:

1. What is satisfying to you or "I feel loved when you . . ."
2. How you try to live it out or "I try to love you by . . ."
3. Some new things you could try or "I believe I could express my love even more by . . ."
4. Some things your partner does that please you or "I feel loved by you when . . ."

That's enough for two or three days. You'll want to intersperse your discussions with some fun activities (where "activities" could also include lying on a beach). And you'll want to conclude your weekend by making a covenant with each other to pursue some of the ideas that emerged from your discussion. Again, always keep in mind that whatever theme you choose, the emphasis should be on enrichment, enjoyment, and fun, not on the resolution of serious problems. You'll want to come back from your weekend with the sense of new life in your marriage.

Grow Spiritually as a Couple

In premarital counseling, we find many Christian couples who tend to take the spiritual aspects of their relationship for granted. And some, who come from differing denominational backgrounds, believe that they can make decisions about church attendance at a later date—after they have worked through what they regard as more pressing challenges.

But spiritual growth is one of the big things in building intimacy. To grow spiritually as a couple means to work as a team in the spiritual development of each of you. In the process, you will not only grow spiritually as individuals but will greatly strengthen the bonds of your union. There are a number of things you can do to grow spiritually as a couple:

1. *Pray together.* At the very least, you can say grace before eating together. You can also pray together in a time of shared devotions, in the morning as a preparation for the day, or in the evening as a benediction on the day and your togetherness.

Prayer is a powerful tool for Christian living. Vic, who is a deacon in his church, has found prayer with his wife, Holly, helpful in all kinds of situations, including one in his church. Vic and Mike, who is also a deacon, had argued vehemently over a church matter. Vic and Holly were so disturbed by the incident that they considered going to a different church:

> We didn't want to leave our church. But I dreaded going to worship and running into Mike. Holly was a great help to me. I know that I obsessed about the disagreement, but she patiently listened to me and struggled with me as I sought some peace in the matter. We also prayed together. For several Sundays in a row, we sat in the car and prayed for God to help me keep my thoughts on worship and solve my difficulties with Mike. And God answered our prayers. Not only was I able to worship and to keep going to church, but Mike and I worked out our differences and are

okay with each other now. And one more thing. I became even more appreciative of Holly and the way she always stands by me.

In the course of growing together as Christians, Vic and Holly are adding a lot of glue to their relationship.

2. *Worship together.* Have you ever sat through a church service and then barely remembered anything that occurred? When life is hectic, when numberless thoughts and concerns are swirling around in your mind, it's difficult to shift mental gears and sit quietly, openly, and alert before God. You can help each other prepare for worship by praying for the service together and then by talking about the various parts of the service (not just the sermon) afterward. Knowing that you are going to discuss the service will help you to focus on it from the start. Among other things, you can talk about which part of the service you found most inspiring, how the music affected you, and how the sermon intersected with your life.

3. *Read the Bible together.* You can map out your own course of study or use one of many devotional aids that offer such things as a passage from the Bible, some reflections, and a suggested prayer. If you develop your own plan of study, concentrate on understanding and applying what you read rather than covering a certain number of verses or chapters. If you use devotional materials, add your own thoughts and interpretations to the written materials. Sharing your insights will strengthen your faith as well as your marriage.

4. *Discuss spiritual matters, including your doubts.* Some of our spiritual forebears would spend Sunday afternoons reading the Bible and discussing spiritual matters. At a minimum, you can do this on your drive home from church services or over Sunday dinner. Perhaps the sermon involved a theological idea that you found stimulating, perplexing, or improbable. The point is, you should be able to discuss spiritual matters with

each other, including your reservations about certain doctrines and practices.

Vic tells how he and Holly have helped each other grow spiritually by their open discussion of both their beliefs and their doubts:

> It's nice when you're like a cheerleading team, agreeing on something. The preacher makes a good point, and we talk about how great it was. Like, in spite of how messed up our world is, we have to keep believing that God is in control. It's also nice when you can share your questions with each other. We've had a few heated debates about spiritual issues. We rarely change each other's mind, but sometimes we do. And no matter, this kind of discussion always makes us feel closer together. Even though we disagree. I guess it's because we *can* disagree and don't have to hide it.

5. *Engage in ministry together.* We strongly believe that every Christian has a ministry—some work that God needs for you to do in what Vic called our "messed up" world. And we also believe that many couples can engage in that ministry as a team. For many years, we have conducted marriage support groups, given seminars and workshops on relationships and other topics, and trained and supervised laypeople as they carry on a caring ministry to individuals in need. For us, this is a shared ministry.

We know of other couples who work together on such things as: regular visits to a Christian orphanage supported by their church; domestic and international mission work; programs to provide temporary housing for the homeless; programs for feeding the homeless on a regular basis; ministry to the ill, the aged, and the bereaved. To be sure, many of these projects require time, perhaps more time than you have available right now. But every church and every charitable organization has need of volunteers and money. You can decide as a couple how much, if any, time you have to offer, and decide as a couple what ministries you will support.

6. *Help each other put experiences into spiritual perspective.* Immersed in the rush of daily life, we can forget that our lives are lived out in the embrace of God. It is well to have regular reminders of, and to interpret our varying experiences in the light of, that fact.

For example, a husband told us how his wife helped him put an anxious time into perspective:

> I had accepted a position in another city. After I made the decision, I began to worry. We barely had enough cash to make the move. What if it didn't work out? What if we couldn't find a suitable place to live? I was really stewing about it when my wife gently reminded me that we had both agreed that this move was God's will for us, and if God was calling us to a new place, God would certainly not strand us once we got there. I remember thinking to myself, "That's right. I've been so bogged down worrying about the move that I forgot about that part."

7. *Model for each other how a Christian lives and relates.* The "fruit of the Spirit is love, joy, peace, patience, kindness, generosity, faithfulness, gentleness, and self-control" (Galatians 5:22-23). Take these qualities one at a time, and spend a week or two cultivating each. We're not suggesting, of course, that you stop the practice after the week or two. In fact, if one of these qualities is tough for you (and if you're like us, most of them will be), you may want to return frequently to give special emphasis to that quality. If this sounds like a lot of work, just

try to envision what it will be like to live with someone who adorns your life with all the fruit of the Spirit. Then, keep at it!

Take Time To . . .

1. Make love. But remind yourselves that "making love" is about more than having sex. It is about caring for each other, respecting each other, helping each other, and building up each other. Start seeing your total life together as opportunities for sensual engagement. If you find the sensual in the routine, you'll also discover it in the bed-room.

2. Plan a special event. It doesn't have to require a lot of money or time—if those are in short supply. But it does have to be something special, and it will take planning. For example, both of you know that you need a weekend away. But you ask: Who's going to take care of the kids? Where can we go that won't require hours of driving time or cost a fortune? Our best solution for handling the kids is to unload them at their grandparents. If this isn't an option for you, work out a deal with friends: They take care of your kids this weekend and you'll take care of theirs one weekend next month. Where to go? We regularly scout the weekend edition of our local newspaper for travel deals. You'll be surprised at how cheaply you can travel if you take advantage of airline and resort specials.

3. Share your spiritual walk with each other. Spiritual matters are often as difficult to talk about openly as are sexual ones. We are afraid of revealing our ignorance or opening ourselves to ridicule and rejection or showing

how inexperienced and naive we actually are. But if your goal is to grow in personal faith and shared intimacy, then open discussion is a must. Sharing your spiritual journey is the most important thing that you can do for your spouse and your relationship.

11

101 Ways To Build Intimacy

"Let marriage be held in honor by all . . ."

Hebrews 13:4

> *"Sometimes I think about the people who gain recognition for great achievements in medicine. That's something I've always wanted to do, but I made the decision early in my career to forego research. I realized that I couldn't do it and still attend to my marriage and family. And I decided that my marriage and my family would never suffer from my ambition. My wife and children have my primary commitment. For me, whatever I have lost in terms of career is nothing compared to what I have gained in love and personal fulfillment."*
>
> *Ben—husband, physician, father*

*G*od helps those who help themselves" is a popular but misleading statement. Our calling is not to self-help but to *self-effort* in the context of God's help—we are told to "work out" our own salvation "for it is God who is at work in you, enabling you both to will and to work for his good pleasure" (Philippians 2:12-13). As you work out your marriage, keep in mind that God is at work in you. And use all the assistance you can find. For God speaks to us in many ways, including the insights and experiences of other people. Exerting effort, using available resources, and letting God work in your life can make the difference between a merely acceptable and an exciting relationship.

We believe that this is the kind of relationship you want, that you have made the important decision to give priority to your marriage, and that you take seriously your calling to hold marriage "in honor" (Hebrews 13:4). Following, therefore, are some practical suggestions for making it happen, a list of 101 ways to develop and maintain intimacy despite your hectic schedules.

Most of the suggestions are inexpensive and require relatively little time. Some will require you to get a baby-sitter if you have children. But all will maintain strong connections, keep romance alive, and say "I love you" in a variety of ways. We have categorized them for quick reference. For example, if you feel that your major problem is that you are surrounded by kids or are pulled by other family demands, look up the suggestions in that category.

We recommend that you make use of the suggestions in all of the categories. Even if some of them do not directly apply to your situation, think about them anyway. Perhaps you can make use of them in some other way. Our purpose here is not only to provide you with some workable activities, but also to stimulate your thinking so that you come up with your own list of unique ideas.

At Any Time or All the Time

1. Don't leave home without giving your spouse a hug and kiss.

2. Break your routine—have leftover pizza for breakfast, sleep in Saturday morning (if the kids will let

you), or have an "instead of" day. For example, *instead* of cleaning, forget the house this week and spend the time having fun together.

3. Give your spouse a daily compliment.

4. Share news of your day's activities with each other.

5. Listen carefully and respond when your spouse tells you something.

6. Do something unexpected—leave a rose on your spouse's pillow, do a task your spouse normally does, or purchase a small gift that is an "I love you" reminder.

7. Hold hands when you walk anywhere.

8. Smile at your spouse frequently—let your smile be a silent "I love you."

9. Play. Be kids at heart. Make a sand castle or a snowman together. Toast marshmallows. Rake a pile of autumn leaves and, then, have fun jumping in them. Play a game of one-on-one basketball.

10. Share in a good deed—wash an elderly person's car, invite a new family to lunch after church, visit someone who's in the hospital, "adopt" a child through one of the many Christian organizations that provide for children throughout the world.

11. Pray together.

12. Worship together.

13. Read and discuss the Bible together.

14. Plan an intimate evening for just the two of you.

15. Tell each other what you dreamed of becoming when you were a child, and talk about your present aspirations.

16. Take a walk together.

17. Get rid of a habit that you know is annoying to your spouse.

18. Take a shower together.

19. Express your appreciation for the tasks your spouse does around the house.

20. Share something humorous with your spouse—set a goal of laughing together every day.

When You Have Just a Few Minutes

21. Leave a love note for your spouse where he or she will find it. Try a soaped message or a sticky note on the bathroom mirror. Tuck one in your partner's briefcase or lunch bag. Or slip one in his or her coat pocket.

22. Send your spouse a valentine even if it's not Valentine's Day.

23. Sing a love song to your spouse via the answering machine. Even if you can't sing, the sentiments will be appreciated.

24. If you're home, take a break, turn on some romantic music, and dance together.

25. Think about one of your spouse's most appealing qualities. And be sure to say "thank you" to him or her for being this kind of person.

26. Call a florist and have flowers delivered to your spouse at work.

27. Write a paragraph that begins, "Something I would love to do with you is . . ." Give it to your spouse later.

28. Sneak up on your spouse and give him or her an unexpected hug and kiss.

When You Have an Hour or Two

29. Start planning for an exotic vacation.

30. Watch a romantic movie together. Keep a few videos on hand for such occasions.

31. Do a spiritual miniretreat. Turn the telephone off, read and discuss some devotional literature, and pray together.

32. Go to a coffeehouse, have a café mocha, and talk about what you would put on your list of "the ten best things we have done together."

33. Cook a romantic dinner together.

34. Cuddle up like spoons and take a nap together.

35. Pick a bouquet of wildflowers or autumn leaves for your spouse.

36. Watch a sunset together.

37. Go out for breakfast together or have a candlelight breakfast at home before the kids wake up.

When You Have an Evening Together

38. Go to a play or a concert. Purchase discount tickets on the day of the event.

39. Take your spouse on a mystery date. The only clues you can provide are what to wear and, if you need to hire a baby-sitter, how late you'll be out.

40. Work together on a home-improvement project you have been wanting to do.

41. Dress up and go to a special restaurant for a leisurely dinner.

42. Dress down, have a light dinner, and then play miniature golf.

43. Try a new activity—go bowling, work out at the gym, browse through books and magazines at a library, attend a lecture, go country western dancing.

44. Have a guilt-free, junk-food night, complete with a favorite comedy double feature via your video recorder.

When You're Surrounded

45. Use your own special code language to send love messages to each other. "I could sure use a sugar fix tonight" can let your mate know that you'd like some extra affection tonight.

46. Have a rule that when your bedroom door is closed, no one enters without knocking and being given permission.

47. Once a week (or as often as fits your schedule), feed the children first, then have a candlelight dinner at home while they do their homework or after they are in bed.

48. Use body language, including touching, to express affection (and to let your children know you are lovers and not merely parents).

49. When you're separated in a crowded room, give your spouse a special smile or a wink.

50. When there are people around, come up behind your spouse and whisper in his or her ear "I love you" or "You're the sexiest person in the room."

51. Compliment your spouse when you are with other people. This will let them know how special your mate is and, at the same time, will tell your spouse how lucky you feel to have him or her in your life.

52. Turn down an invitation to a party, meeting, or family gathering and reserve the evening for you and your spouse.

When Your Marriage Needs a Shot in the Arm

53. Attend a funny movie or play, have a late dinner afterward, and talk about your funniest experiences as a couple.

54. Get out your wedding pictures and relive the experience.

55. Take turns giving each other a back rub or body massage.

56. Do something really adventurous together. Try your hand at skiing, rock climbing, white-water rafting, or bungee jumping for a *real* change!

57. Plan a surprise romantic weekend for your spouse. Take care of all the details: Make the reservations, get a friend or relatives to watch the children, pack the suitcases, and then spring the surprise on your spouse.

58. Sit down, hold hands, look in each other's eyes, and tell each other in detail everything you like, value, and appreciate about the other.

59. Declare a "love day." For twenty-four hours, don't nag or complain about what your spouse does or doesn't do; instead, shower him or her with affection.

60. Make a list of three things that your spouse could do to make your relationship more romantic. Trade lists and, then, each of you do the things on your mate's list during the next three weeks.

61. Develop a new interest or hobby together. The possibilities are endless, ranging from stamp collecting to hang gliding.

62. Spend a night at a motel. Bring candles and romantic music.

When You're Apart for the Day

63. Telephone your spouse at work or at home just to see how he or she is doing and to say "I love you" and "I can't wait to see you!"

64. Keep a picture of your spouse and family close by. Throw them kisses throughout the day.

65. Make a mental or written note of interesting or humorous things that happen so you can share them when you get home.

66. Put a chocolate kiss in your spouse's briefcase.

67. Pick up a thoughtful surprise—a book by her favorite author, a box of his favorite chocolates—for your mate when you're on your lunch break.

68. Make a date to have lunch with your spouse.

69. When you reunite at the end of the day, greet each other with a hug and kiss and words that say how happy you are to be back together.

When You Have to Be Away for Days

70. Plan to spend some special time together before you part. The memories of these moments will keep you united while you're separated.

71. Leave a note, where your spouse can find it after you're gone, that says how much you are looking forward to being together again.

72. Send a postcard home each day with a love message on it.

73. Keep in touch in some way each day—by telephone or E-mail.

74. Begin each day with a prayer of gratitude and a request for God to watch over your family.

75. Use any spare time when you're apart to learn something new or grow in some way; share what you have learned with each other after you are back together.

76. Send your spouse a customized greeting card.

77. Plan for a special homecoming. Keep it low key because reentry is often exhausting. But also make it memorable so that each of you knows how much the other was missed.

When Money Is Tight

78. Have a picnic in the park.

79. Invite several couples for a potluck dinner.

80. Make a list of everything in your community that is free. Consult it and update it frequently.

81. Turn the lights off and cuddle in the dark.

82. Over dinner, talk about the idea that "the best things in life are free." Express gratitude for such things in your own life.

83. Jog around the local high school track.

84. Make a bowl of popcorn and watch TV.

85. Try to maintain a good mood; a happy person is a priceless gift for your spouse.

When You're Weary

86. Give your spouse, or ask your spouse to give you, a couple of free hours to take a nap.

87. Go to bed early, and chat until you are drowsy.

88. Take a stroll together—mild exercise can reenergize you.

89. Regularly schedule some individual private time.

90. Bring dinner in instead of cooking and use the time saved to sit and talk.

91. Take a slow bubble bath.

92. Sit side by side while each of you reads a good book.

93. Give each other a foot massage.

When You Want to Do Something Special

94. Cook your spouse's favorite meal.

95. Become a part of a couples' group in your church.

96. Go away for a do-it-yourself marriage enrichment weekend.

97. Pretend that you are on a first date and treat each other accordingly.

98. Enroll in an adult education class together.

99. Talk—really talk—about the future of your relationship. Discuss your hopes and aspirations and set specific goals about where you want to be in five, ten, and twenty years.

100. Volunteer for a mission trip sponsored by your church or another group.

101. Plan your dream vacation—set a definite date and work out what you need to do in order to make it happen.

Now it's your turn. Use your imagination and understanding of your personal needs and preferences to add to this list. Even the busiest couples can find things to do that will fit into their schedules and strengthen their relationship. Your marriage is worth the effort!